Better Homes and Gardens

Stitching Pretty

101 Lovely Cross-Stitch Projects to Make

Better Homes and Gardens® Books
Des Moines, Iowa

Better Homes and Gardens® Books
An Imprint of Meredith® Books

Stitching Pretty

Editor: Carol Field Dahlstrom
Technical Editor: Susan M. Banker
Graphic Designer: Angela Haupert Hoogensen
Copy Chief: Terri Fredrickson
Copy and Production Editor: Victoria Forlini
Editorial Operations Manager: Karen Schirm
Managers, Book Production: Pam Kvitne, Marjorie J. Schenkelberg
Contributing Copy Editor: Chardel Blaine
Contributing Proofreaders: Becky Danley, Karen Brewer Grossman, Margaret Smith
Photographer: Andy Lyons CameraWorks
Technical Illustrator: Chris Neubauer Graphics, Inc.
Electronic Production Coordinator: Paula Forest
Editorial and Design Assistants: Kaye Chabot, Mary Lee Gavin

Meredith® Books
Editor in Chief: James D. Blume
Design Director: Matt Strelecki
Managing Editor: Gregory H. Kayko

Director, Sales, Special Markets: Rita McMullen
Director, Sales, Premiums: Michael A. Peterson
Director, Sales, Retail: Tom Wierzbicki
Director, Book Marketing: Brad Elmitt
Director, Operations: George A. Susral
Director, Production: Douglas M. Johnston
Vice President and General Manager: Douglas J. Guendel

Better Homes and Gardens® **Magazine**
Editor in Chief: Karol DeWulf Nickell

Meredith Publishing Group
President, Publishing Group: Stephen M. Lacy
Vice President-Publishing Director: Bob Mate

Meredith Corporation
Chairman and Chief Executive Officer: William T. Kerr

Chairman of the Executive Committee: E. T. Meredith III

Contents

The stitches of today...
create the memories
for a lifetime

It's a wonderful thing to create a cherished work of art by simply using a needle and embroidery floss. Although the supplies are few, the process is quite magical as a soft piece of cloth transforms from a solid swatch into a canvas of colorful design.

The technique of cross-stitch is just as beautiful as what it produces. The process calms the senses as one lovingly stitches along, watching the story unfold. And while the art form warrents patience, accuracy, and creativity, it is treasured for its intricacy and personal expression.

Cross-stitch is a time-honored craft that continues to be loved all around the world both by those who stitch and those who simply admire the work of others. The chapters of this book celebrate that love of cross-stitch with a variety of timeless designs.

Throughout the pages are designs for last-minute gifts, home decor pieces, samplers to commemorate special events, and much more. Each project is accompanied by an easy-to-read chart, key, and complete instructions. There are also several stitch diagrams and helpful tips to ensure the success of each project.

No matter which design you choose to stitch first, you'll surely find dozens more to add to your never-ending "can't-wait-to-do" list. Here's hoping you find new designs you'll soon call favorites and that each stitch is done with confidence and love.

Happy stitching,

Carol Field Dahlstrom

Forever
Keepsakes

*Within our lives are
images that are timeless,
such as the innocent look of a child,
the natural wonders that surround
us, and the heartfelt joy that
Christmas brings. These earthly
gifts and more are celebrated in
this chapter's treasured cross-stitch
collection. Each of the keepsake
designs is beautifully framed
to cherish today and for
generations to come.*

*Surrounded by a variety of
single-stem flowers, a basket of
fruit takes center stage in this
sampler. Although beautiful
framed, the individual motifs
could be stitched separately for
smaller projects.*

Bounty & Blooms

MATERIALS

FABRIC
14×14-inch piece of 28-count
light blue Jobelan

FLOSS
Cotton embroidery floss in colors listed in key

SUPPLIES
Needle; embroidery hoop; desired mat and frame

INSTRUCTIONS

Tape or zigzag the edges of the fabric to prevent fraying. Find center of chart and center of fabric; begin stitching there. Use three plies of floss to work cross-stitches over two threads of fabric. Work backstitches using one ply of floss. Press the finished stitchery from the back. Mat and frame as desired.

ANCHOR		DMC
1046	⌗	435 Chestnut
256	▽	704 Chartreuse
590	•	712 Cream
326	○	720 Bittersweet
305	+	725 Topaz
9575	△	758 Light terra-cotta
307	=	783 Christmas gold
907	⋈	832 Bronze
360	■	839 Beige-brown
257	✕	905 Parrot green
1034	◨	931 Antique blue
268	▲	937 Pine green
186	‖	959 Medium aqua
1015	✳	3777 Deep terra-cotta
1076	✲	3814 Aquamarine
279	⁄	3819 Moss green
891	⊟	3822 Straw
339	◎	3830 Terra-cotta
324	◠	3853 Autumn gold

BACKSTITCH (1X)

862	╱	934 Deep pine green – all stitches

Stitch count: 100 high x 102 wide
Finished design sizes:
28-count fabric – 7 x 7¼ inches
32-count fabric – 6¼ x 6⅜ inches
36-count fabric – 5½ x 5¾ inches

Miss Lizzy

Surrounded by strawberries highlighted with seed beads, this sweet young lady prepares for a special Sunday outing. The key is below; the chart is on pages 12–13.

the chart is on pages 12–13.

MATERIALS

FABRIC
20×14-inch piece of 14-count white Aida cloth

FLOSS
Cotton embroidery floss in colors listed in key
1 additional skein of white (DMC 000)

SUPPLIES
Needle
Embroidery hoop
Seed beads in colors listed in key
Desired mat and frame

INSTRUCTIONS

Tape or zigzag edges of fabric to prevent fraying. Find center of chart and center of fabric; begin stitching there.

Use three plies of floss to work cross-stitches. Work blended needle and backstitches as specified in key. Attach beads using one ply of floss.

Press finished stitchery from the back. Mat and frame design as desired.

MISS LIZZY

ANCHOR		DMC
002	•	000 White
038	★	335 Medium rose
310	#	434 Medium chestnut
1046	◪	435 Dark chestnut
1045	●	436 Dark tan
362	◩	437 Medium tan
361	+	738 Light tan
885	▽	739 Pale tan
302	I	743 Yellow
1022	⊡	760 Salmon
024	✕	776 Pink
359	■	801 Coffee brown
1044	▲	895 Hunter green
052	◉	899 Light rose
244	◇	987 Medium forest green
242	☆	989 Pale forest green
1009	△	3770 True ivory
177	✳	3807 Cornflower blue

Stitch count: 201 high x 127 wide
Finished design sizes:
14-count fabric – 14½ x 9⅛ inches
11-count fabric –18⅜ x 11⅝ inches
18-count fabric –11¼ x 7⅛ inches

ANCHOR		DMC
BLENDED NEEDLE		
002	⧄	000 White (1X) and
398		415 Pearl gray (1X)
882	◆	758 Terra-cotta (1X) and
881		945 Dark ivory (1X)
881	−	945 Dark ivory (1X) and
1010		951 Medium ivory (1X)
BEADS		
038	⊙	335 Medium rose and 00968 Red Mill Hill seed bead
024	◎	776 Pink and 02005 Dusty rose Mill Hill seed bead
BACKSTITCH		
038	╱	335 Medium rose–dress (1X)
235	╱	414 Steel–flowers, blouse, and petticoats (1X)
310	╱	434 Medium chestnut–hair and tendrils (2X)
1046	╱	435 Dark chestnut–skin, facial details, and hat (1X)
1022	╱	760 Salmon–lips (1X)
1044	╱	895 Hunter green–leaves and stems (1X)
177	╱	3807 Cornflower blue–iris of eye (1X)

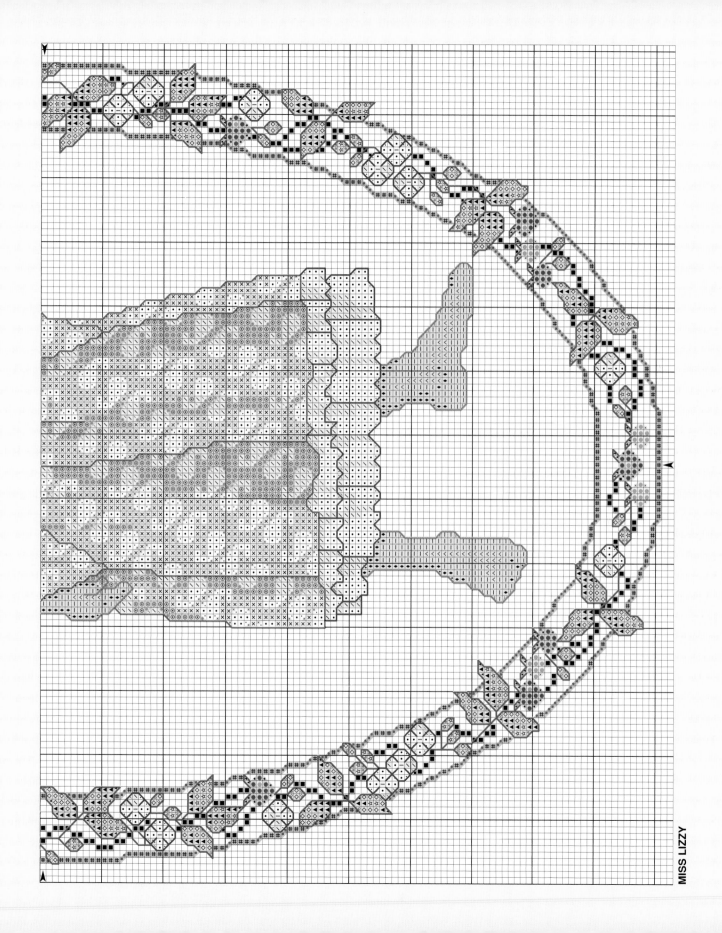

MISS LIZZY

Miss Ginna

Complement Miss Lizzy, page 10, with the portrait of her sister, Miss Ginna, surrounded by seed-bead grapes. The key is below; the chart appears on pages 16–17.

MATERIALS

FABRIC
20×14-inch piece of 14-count white Aida cloth

FLOSS
Cotton embroidery floss in colors listed in key
1 additional skein of white (DMC 000)

SUPPLIES
Needle
Embroidery hoop
Seed beads in colors listed in key
Desired mat and frame

INSTRUCTIONS

Tape or zigzag edges of fabric to prevent fraying. Find center of chart and center of fabric; begin stitching there.

Use three plies of floss to work cross-stitches. Work blended needle as specified in key. Work backstitches and attach beads using one ply of floss.

Press finished stitchery from the back. Mat and frame design as desired.

MISS GINNA

ANCHOR		DMC
002	⊡	000 White
1025	▲	347 Deep salmon
310	✕	434 Chestnut
362	◇	437 Tan
1022	−	760 True salmon
1021	○	761 Light salmon
177	■	792 Dark cornflower blue
176	☆	793 Medium cornflower blue
175	△	794 Light cornflower blue
1044	◆	895 Hunter green
360	★	898 Coffee brown
244	▣	987 Medium forest green
242	▯	989 Pale forest green
1023	◩	3712 Medium salmon

BLENDED NEEDLE

ANCHOR		DMC
387	◺	Ecru (1X) and
1009		3770 True ivory (1X)
002	S	000 White (1X) and
398		415 Pearl gray (1X)
002	♡	000 White (1X) and
175		794 Light cornflower blue (1X)
1025	▣	347 Deep salmon (1X) and
1023		3712 Medium salmon (1X)

ANCHOR		DMC
1022	◎	760 True salmon (1X) and
881		945 Dark ivory (1X)
881	⊞	945 Dark ivory (1X) and
1010		951 Medium ivory (1X)

BACKSTITCH

ANCHOR		DMC
002	╱	000 White–eye highlights
400	╱	317 Pewter–collar, cuff, and towel
1025	╱	347 Deep salmon–hair ribbon
310	╱	434 Chestnut–hair
362	╱	437 Tan–legs, arms, face, and nose
175	╱	794 Light cornflower blue–hat
127	╱	823 Navy–dress and hat
1044	╱	895 Hunter green–leaves
360	╱	898 Coffee brown–hair, eyes, basket and vines inside oval
1023	╱	3712 Medium salmon–mouth

BEADS

ANCHOR		DMC
045	⦿	814 Dark garnet and 03033 Claret Mill Hill Antique seed bead
043	⦿	815 Medium garnet and 03034 Royal Amethyst Mill Hill Antique seed bead
127	⦿	823 Navy and 03002 Midnight Mill Hill Antique seed bead

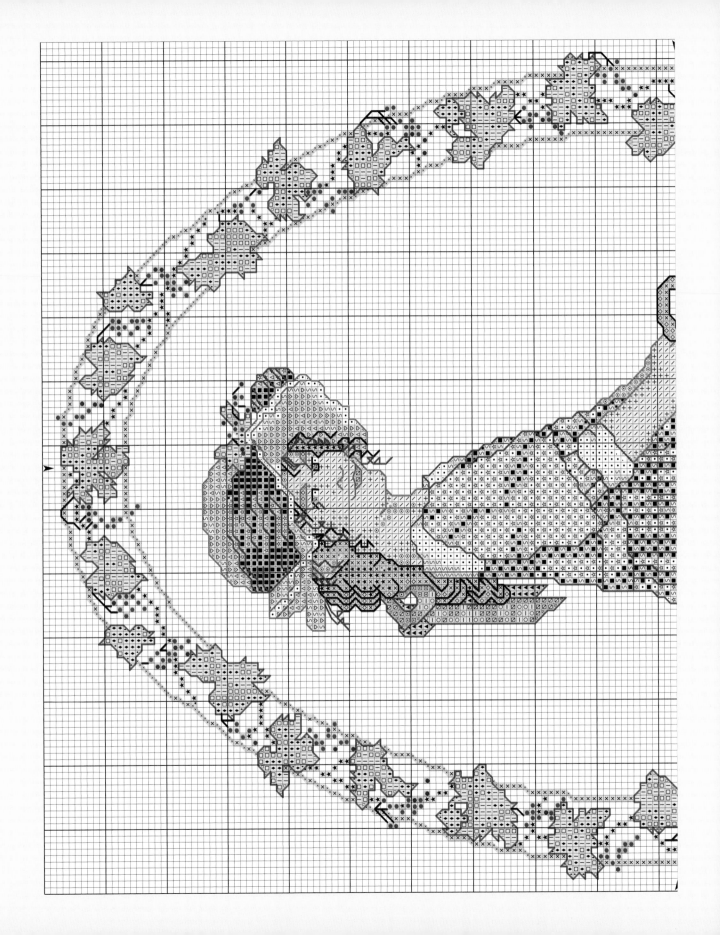

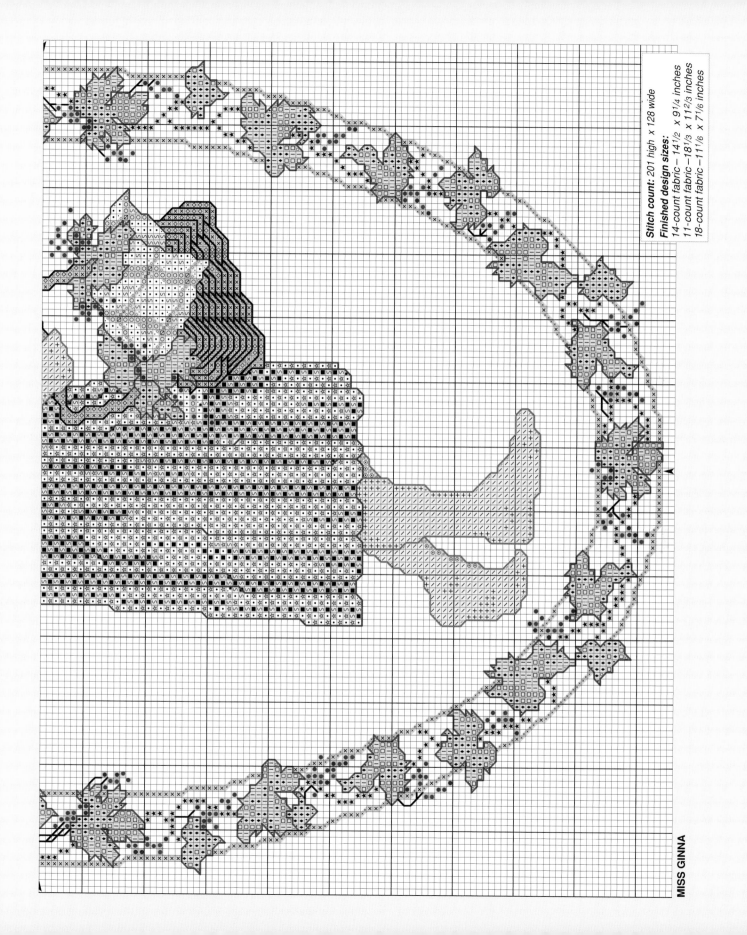

Stitch count: 201 high x 128 wide

Finished design sizes:
14-count fabric – 14½ x 9¼ inches
11-count fabric – 18⅓ x 11⅔ inches
18-count fabric – 11⅙ x 7⅙ inches

MISS GINNA

These vintage teddy bears share a deep unconditional love. Charles and Willy are brothers modeled after bears from the early 20th century.

Brother Bears

MATERIALS

FABRIC
12×10-inch piece of 18-count sweetbrier Heartsong fabric

FLOSS
Cotton embroidery floss and metallic thread in colors listed in key

SUPPLIES
Needle; embroidery hoop Desired mat and frame

INSTRUCTIONS

Tape or zigzag edges of fabric. Find center of chart and of fabric; begin stitching there. Use three plies of floss to work cross-stitches over one thread of fabric. Work backstitches using one ply unless otherwise specified in key. Satin-stitch the nose in the direction indicated by the symbol on the chart. Press stitchery from back. Mat and frame.

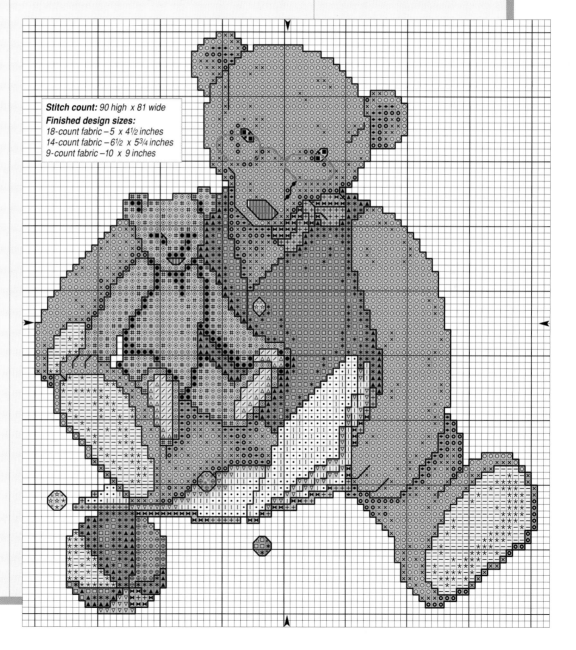

Stitch count: *90 high x 81 wide*
Finished design sizes:
18-count fabric – 5 x 4½ inches
14-count fabric – 6½ x 5¾ inches
9-count fabric – 10 x 9 inches

ANCHOR		DMC	
002	·	000	White
352	◉	300	Deep mahogany
1049	✕	301	Medium mahogany
403	■	310	Black
214	✚	368	Pistachio
362	✴	437	Tan
903	⊞	640	Beige gray
301	☆	744	Yellow
234	❘	762	Pearl gray
360	◆	898	Coffee brown
897	▲	902	Garnet
1034	⊕	931	Medium antique blue
1033	◇	932	True antique blue
1010	─	951	Ivory
1002	○	977	Golden brown
899	◉	3023	Light brown gray
397	╱	3024	Pale brown gray
360	●	3031	Deep mocha
903	△	3032	Medium mocha
870	▽	3042	Antique violet
1024	□	3328	Salmon
263	⋈	3362	Loden
1015	✽	3777	Terra cotta

SATIN STITCH
403	❘	310	Black – bear noses (3X)

BACKSTITCH
1049	╱	301	Medium mahogany – little bear's eyes (2X)
403	╱	310	Black – claws (2X)
382	╱	3371	Black brown – all remaining stitches
	╱	001	Kreinik silver cable – eye glasses (2X)

Majestic Rooster

This exotic rooster stands with his head held high next to a tree stump entwined with blooming strawberries. A rich blue linen background emphasizes his aristocratic features. The key is below; the chart is on pages 22–23.

MATERIALS

FABRIC
18×16-inch piece of 28-count Nordic blue linen

FLOSS
Cotton embroidery floss in colors listed in key

SUPPLIES
Needle
Embroidery hoop
Desired mat and frame

INSTRUCTIONS

Tape or zigzag the edges of the Nordic blue linen to prevent fraying. Find center of the chart and the center of the fabric; begin stitching rooster there.

Use two plies of floss to work the cross-stitches over two threads of blue linen. Work all backstitches using one ply of floss.

Press the finished stitchery from the back. Mat and frame as desired.

MAJESTIC ROOSTER

ANCHOR	DMC		ANCHOR	DMC		ANCHOR	DMC
002	· 000 White		305	∼ 725 True topaz		397	‖ 3024 Pale brown gray
403	■ 310 Black		293	− 727 Pale topaz		871	✳ 3041 Medium antique violet
9046	♥ 321 Christmas red		890	═ 729 Medium old gold		870	◩ 3042 Light antique violet
013	▢ 349 Dark coral		275	I 746 Off white		847	⁄ 3072 Beaver gray
011	▽ 350 Medium coral		307	★ 783 Christmas gold		268	⊙ 3345 Medium hunter green
374	✚ 420 Medium hazel		013	◆ 817 Deep coral		817	✕ 3346 Light hunter green
267	⊛ 470 Medium avocado		944	★ 869 Dark hazel		264	◇ 3347 Yellow green
266	◿ 471 Light avocado		035	◈ 891 Dark carnation		872	▼ 3740 Dark antique violet
253	◺ 472 Pale avocado		027	⊖ 894 Pale carnation		1050	● 3781 Mocha
046	◪ 666 Red		1044	▲ 895 Dark hunter green		273	◢ 3787 Dark brown gray
891	○ 676 Light old gold		861	⋈ 935 Pine green		**BACKSTITCH**	
886	✛ 677 Pale old gold		393	◆ 3022 Medium brown gray		382	╱ 3371 Black brown – all stitches
901	△ 680 Dark old gold		899	☆ 3023 Light brown gray			

MAJESTIC ROOSTER stitch count:
139 high x 104 wide
MAJESTIC ROOSTER finished design sizes:
14-count fabric – 10 x 7½ inches
11-count fabric – 12⅝ x 9½ inches
16-count fabric – 8⅝ x 6½ inches

MAJESTIC ROOSTER

Christmas Bells

A familiar Christmas carol inspired this elegant holiday design. Simple cross-stitches form the quaint architectural lines of a row of steeples. Algerian eyelets add dimension to the bell towers. Gold seed beads provide the perfect finishing touch.

MATERIALS

FABRIC
14×14-inch piece of 32-count white linen

FLOSS
*Cotton embroidery floss in colors listed in key
on page 27*

SUPPLIES
*Embroidery hoop; needle
Gold seed beads
Desired mat and frame*

INSTRUCTIONS

Tape or zigzag the edges of the fabric. Find the center of the chart, *page 26,* and of fabric; begin stitching there.

Use two plies of floss to work cross-stitches over two threads of fabric. Using the diagrams, *below,* work Smryna cross-stitches, long-armed cross-stitches, and blended needle as specified in key on *page 27.* Use two plies to work eyelets unless otherwise specified in key. For eyelets, give each stitch a tug to open a small hole. Work backstitches using one ply. Attach beads using one ply.

Press the finished stitchery from the back. Mat and frame as desired.

Smyrna Cross-Stitch

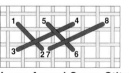

Long-Armed Cross-Stitch

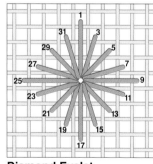

Diamond Eyelet

Algerian Eyelet

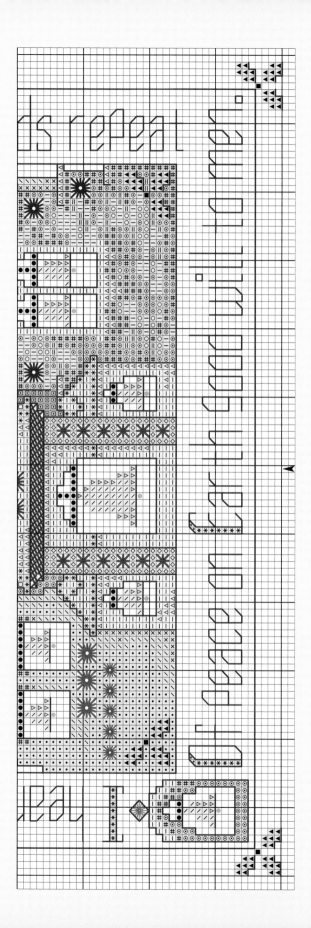

CHRISTMAS BELLS

ANCHOR		DMC	
399	◁	318	Steel
1025	■	347	Salmon
1047	‖	402	Mahogany
398	I	415	Pearl gray
877	✕	502	Medium blue green
875	•	503	True blue green
898	●	611	Drab brown
923	◀	699	Christmas green
907	▷	832	Bronze
850	□	926	Medium gray blue
848	‖	927	Light gray blue
4146	▬	950	Light rose beige
779	✱	3768	Dark gray blue
1007	#	3772	Cocoa
1008	⊙	3773	Medium rose beige
1013	○	3778	Terra-cotta
876	╱	3816	Celadon green
874	╱	3822	Straw

BLENDED NEEDLE

398	⊡	415	Pearl gray (1X) and
869		3743	Antique violet (1X)
398	◇	415	Pearl gray (1X) and
886		3047	Yellow beige (1X)

ANCHOR		DMC	
LONG-ARMED CROSS-STITCH			
398	✕✕	415	Pearl gray (1X)
BLENDED LONG-ARMED CROSS-STITCH			
398	✕✕	415	Pearl gray (1X) and
886		3047	Yellow beige (1X)
DIAMOND EYELETS			
907	✴	832	Bronze (2X)
ALGERIAN EYELETS			
398	✳	415	Pearl gray
875	✳	503	True blue green
1007	✳	3772	Cocoa
BLENDED ALGERIAN EYELETS			
398	✳	415	Pearl gray (1X) and
869		3743	Antique violet (1X)
398	✳	415	Pearl gray (1X) and
886		3047	Yellow beige (1X)
BLENDED SMYRNA CROSS STITCH			
398	✳	415	Pearl gray (1X) and
886		3047	Yellow beige (1X)
BACKSTITCH			
236	╱	3799	Charcoal– all stitches

ANCHOR		DMC	
BEADS			
	●	00557	Gold Mill Hill seed beads

Stitch count: 131 high x 119 wide

Finished design sizes:
16-count fabric – 8 x 7³/₈ inches
14-count fabric – 9¹/₄ x 8¹/₂ inches
18-count fabric – 7¹/₄ x 6⁵/₈ inches

Gloria Sampler

The radiance of the Christmas season is reflected in this elegant sampler. The simple lines of this exquisite design are accented with sparkling threads and glittering seed beads. The key is below, the chart is on pages 30–31.

The key is below, the chart is on pages 30–31.

MATERIALS

FABRIC
16½×15-inch piece of 14-count white Aida cloth

FLOSS
Cotton embroidery floss in colors listed in key
Blending filament in colors listed in key

SUPPLIES
Embroidery hoop
Needle
Gold seed beads
Desired mat and frame

INSTRUCTIONS

Tape or zigzag edges of fabric. Find center of chart and center of fabric; begin stitching there.

Work all blended needle cross-stitches as specified in key. Work backstitches using one ply of floss. Sew beads to design as indicated on chart using one ply of bronze (DMC 832) floss.

Press the finished stitchery from the back. Mat and frame as desired.

O GLORIA SAMPLER

ANCHOR		DMC
BLENDED NEEDLE		
110	◆	208 Lavender (2X) and
		026 Kreinik amethyst blending filament (1X)
403	■	310 Black (2X) and
		005 Kreinik black blending filament (1X)
400	▲	317 Pewter (2X) and
		025 Kreinik gray blending filament (1X)
399	✕	318 Steel (2X) and
		025 Kreinik gray blending filament (1X)
234	Ⅰ	762 Pearl gray (2X) and
		001 Kreinik silver blending filament (1X)
045	✚	814 Garnet (2X) and
		003 Kreinik red blending filament (1X)
907	◯	832 Bronze (2X) and
		002 Kreinik gold blending filament (1X)
246	⬤	986 Forest green (2X) and
		008 Kreinik green blending filament (1X)
BACKSTITCH		
403	╱	310 Black—all stitches
BEADS		
	•	00557 Mill Hill gold glass seed bead

Stitch count: 141 high x 119 wide
Finished design sizes:
14-count fabric – 10 x 8½ inches
11-count fabric – 12⅞ x 10⅞ inches
18-count fabric – 7⅞ x 6⅝ inches

© GLORIA SAMPLER

Tokens of Love

When you want to stitch something for someone you love, you will be inspired by the endearing designs in this chapter. Whether you are looking for a floral wedding sampler, a heart-filled motif for your dear mother or grandmother, or a sentimental verse destined to become a family heirloom, you are sure to find a new favorite here. Whichever project you choose, put love into every stitch.

*This heart-filled sampler is
brimming with romantic designs
to stitch and give with love.*

Endearing Sampler

MATERIALS

FABRIC
14×14-inch piece of 28-count
light gray Jobelan

FLOSS
Cotton embroidery floss in colors listed in key

SUPPLIES
Needle; embroidery hoop; desired mat and frame

INSTRUCTIONS

Tape or zigzag fabric edges.
Find center of chart and of
fabric; begin stitching there.

Use three plies
of floss to work
cross-stitches over
two threads of
fabric. Work
straight stitches
and backstitches
using one ply.
Press stitchery
from back.
Mat and frame
as desired.

ANCHOR		DMC
002	•	000 White
110	⊞	209 Medium lavender
342	○	211 Pale lavender
233	▽	451 Dark shell gray
231	I	453 Light shell gray
063	◉	602 Medium cranberry
062	+	603 True cranberry
074	−	605 Pale cranberry
256	II	704 Chartreuse
295	∧	726 Topaz
303	✳	742 Tangerine
177	▲	3839 Medium lavender-blue
120	✕	3840 Light lavender-blue

BACKSTITCH

110	/	208 Dark lavender – purple ribbons, pansies
1041	/	535 Ash gray (2X) – doves, top center heart
1041	/	535 Ash gray (1X) – doves, LOVE
063	/	602 Medium cranberry – hearts, pink flowers
122	/	792 Cornflower blue – blue ribbon, blue heart
257	/	905 Parrot green – stems

STRAIGHT STITCH

303	/	742 Tangerine – dove beaks

FRENCH KNOT (1X wrapped twice)

1041	●	535 Ash gray – dove eyes

LAZY DAISY STITCH

257	⟋	905 Parrot green – pink flower petals

Stitch count: 101 high x 101 wide

Finished design sizes:
28-count fabric – 7⅛ x 7⅛ inches
32-count fabric – 6⅜ x 6⅜ inches
36-count fabric – 5⅔ x 5⅔ inches

Camellias & Hearts

This sentimental cross-stitch piece celebrates the beauty of camellias and hearts with plenty of pattern, rich color, and texture.

MATERIALS

FABRIC
13×14-inch piece of 14-count white Aida cloth

FLOSS
Cotton embroidery floss in colors listed in key
#8 gold braid

SUPPLIES
Needle; embroidery hoop; seed beads in colors listed in key; desired mat and frame

INSTRUCTIONS

Tape or zigzag fabric edges. Find center of chart and of fabric; begin stitching there. Use three plies of floss or one strand of braid to work cross-stitches. Work backstitches using one ply. Use one ply to attach beads. Press stitchery from back. Frame as desired.

ANCHOR	DMC	
878	■	501 Blue-green
212	✳	561 Dark seafoam
208	○	563 True seafoam
062	+	603 True cranberry
055	△	604 Light cranberry
050	＝	605 Pale cranberry
275	•	746 Off-white
246	▲	986 Dark forest green
243	□	988 Light forest green
292	╱	3078 Pale lemon
	✕	002 Kreinik gold #8 braid

BACKSTITCH

380	╱	838 Beige-brown – corner boxes, outline of rectangle, and flowers (1X)
246	╱	986 Dark forest green – vines (1X)
	╱	002 Kreinik gold #8 braid – lattice background (1X)

MILL HILL BEADS

- 00479 White seed bead
- 00553 Old rose seed bead
- 02005 Dusty rose seed bead
- 02012 Royal plum seed bead
- 03003 Antique cranberry seed bead
- 03034 Royal amethyst seed bead

Stitch count: 92 high x 110 wide
Finished design sizes:
14-count fabric – 6 5/8 x 7 7/8 inches
11-count fabric – 8 3/8 x 10 inches
18-count fabric – 5 x 6 inches

Love Always

Silk thread is a luxury every stitcher loves. It is one of the most beautiful fibers available and the wonderfully smooth silk thread texture slips through fabric with ease. Use a sampling of several silk threads to stitch this pretty heart and you'll find yourself wanting to stitch everything with silk. The chart and key are on page 41.

MATERIALS

FABRIC
18×18-inch piece of 20-count black Jobelan
12×12-inch piece of black felt

FLOSS
Mori in color listed in key on page 41
Soie d'Alger in colors listed in key
Silk Serica in color listed in key
Soie Perlee in color listed in key

SUPPLIES
Needle
Embroidery hoop
Erasable fabric marker
Tracing paper
12×12-inch piece of foam-covered self-stick
mounting board
Crafts glue
2 yards of purchased ⅜-inch-diameter rose
satin cording
1¼ yards of 2-inch-wide pregathered pink lace
2 purchased periwinkle tassels

INSTRUCTIONS

Tape or zigzag edges of Jobelan to prevent fraying. Find the center of the chart and the center of the fabric; begin stitching there.

Use two plies of Mori or Soie d'Alger to work cross-stitches over two threads of fabric. Using the stitch diagrams on *page 41*, work Smyrna cross-stitches using one strand of Soie Perlee. Use one strand of Serica to work satin stitches. If desired, gently dampen Serica satin stitches with a damp cloth and allow to dry. Place the finished piece, facedown, on a soft towel and press.

Use an erasable fabric marker to draw the outline of a heart about ½ inch beyond the stitching. Place tracing paper on top of the fabric and trace heart outline. Cut out and use as a pattern to cut one heart shape from mounting board and one from felt. Cut out Jobelan heart ½ inch beyond the marker line.

Remove paper from mounting board and position fabric on foam side. Fold excess fabric to the wrong side and glue it in place.

Cut enough cording to go around the heart shape. Glue in place, folding ends to back. Glue lace behind cording. Tie a bow in center of remaining cording. Glue one end to each rounded edge at top of heart. Glue felt heart to back. Tie tassels onto bow.

ABOUT SILK THREADS

Silk fibers come from the cocoon of a moth caterpillar, which is native to China. Because the fibers are translucent, they reflect light, resulting in a lustrous, shimmering thread. Silk fibers absorb dye better than any other natural fiber, resulting in richly colored threads. Silk thread is stronger than an equal thickness of cotton, lighter in weight, and has a smooth texture that easily pulls through cross-stitch and needlepoint fabrics.

Two categories of silk thread are available to cross-stitchers.

Filament silk is made from the long fibers unwound from the cocoon. It has a very high luster—perfect for satin and other long stitches.

- *Soie Perlee* and *Soie Gobelins* are firmly twisted, much like pearl cotton. Soie Perlee is similar in diameter to #8 pearl cotton and Soie Gobelins compares to #12 pearl.

- *Silk Serica* and *Ping Ling* have a low twist and can be separated easily—Serica into three individual strands, Ping Ling into six plies.

- *Soie Platte* is untwisted and ribbonlike in appearance. Composed of extremely fine strands that can be separated, it has a very high luster.

Spun silk is made from fibers that have been broken and spun together to form a continuous thread, creating a very soft, polished appearance.

- *Soie d'Alger* is seven-ply silk that is practically interchangeable with floss and available in 400 colors.

- *Mori* is a six-ply silk, slightly fluffier than Soie d'Alger and dyed to perfectly match Serica.

- *Soie Noppee* is a thick single strand with a furry appearance.

LOVE ALWAYS
KREINIK SILK THREAD
- **1032 Pink Mori**
▲ **2944 Rose Soie d'Alger**
✗ **4913 Periwinkle Soie d'Alger**
SATIN STITCH
| **1032 Pink Serica**
SMYRNA CROSS STITCH
※ **2944 Rose Soie Perlee**
BACKSTITCH
| **4913 Periwinkle Soie d'Alger**
Stitch count: 101 high x 122 wide
Finished design sizes:
10-count fabric – 10 x 12 inches
11-count fabric – 9¼ x 11⅛ inches
14-count fabric – 7¼ x 8⅞ inches

Let Mother know you care by stitching her a gift of love. Our sweet Mother's Sampler is worked on 28-count ivory Jobelan fabric destined to become a splendid tribute to cherish forever.

Mother's Sampler

MATERIALS

FABRIC
12½×10-inch piece of 28-count ivory Jobelan fabric

FLOSS
Cotton embroidery floss in colors listed in key

SUPPLIES
Needle; embroidery hoop; desired mat and frame

INSTRUCTIONS

Tape or zigzag fabric edges. Find center of chart and of fabric; begin stitching there. Use three plies of floss to work cross-stitches over two threads of fabric. Work backstitches using one ply. Press stitchery from back. Mat and frame as desired.

ANCHOR		DMC
891	⊡	676 Light old gold
886	I	677 Pale old gold
161	▽	813 Powder blue
162	✕	826 Bright blue
229	●	910 True emerald
209	☐	912 Light emerald
203	✶	954 Nile green
075	◆	962 Medium rose pink
025	⊙	3716 Light rose pink

BACKSTITCH

162	╱	826 Bright blue–lettering
360	╱	839 Beige brown–bird's beak, eye, and feet
075	╱	962 Medium rose pink–heart

Stitch count: 107 high x 69 wide

Finished design sizes:
14-count fabric – 7⅝ x 5 inches
11-count fabric – 9¾ x 6¼ inches
16-count fabric – 6⅝ x 4⅜ inches

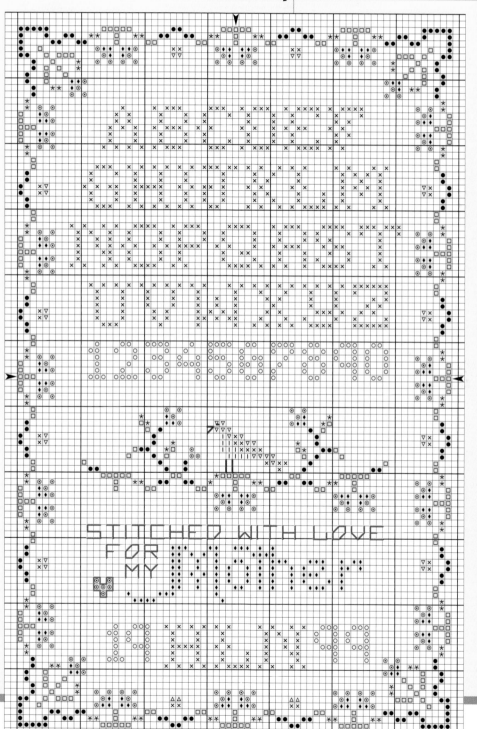

Ribbon & Roses Wedding

A delicate pearl border frames the pastel floss shades of our elegant bridal sampler. The matching rice bag is trimmed in lace and satin pastel ribbons to hold tiny treasures. Shoe clips, stitched with a single rose motif, are perfect accessories for the bride and her bridesmaids. Stitch another single rose on a purchased handkerchief as a special gift for the mothers of the bride and groom. The charts and key are on pages 46–47.

MATERIALS
FOR THE SAMPLER

FABRIC
18×15-inch piece of 28-count new khaki Brittney fabric

FLOSS
Cotton embroidery floss in colors listed in key on page 46

SUPPLIES
*Needle; embroidery hoop
2½-millimeter pearls
White sewing thread; desired mat and frame*

INSTRUCTIONS
FOR THE SAMPLER

Tape or zigzag the edges of the fabric to prevent fraying. Find center of chart and of fabric; begin stitching there.

Use two plies of floss to work cross-stitches over two threads of fabric. Work straight stitches of border using one ply of floss. Work backstitches using one ply of floss. Use sewing thread to sew pearls to fabric at positions shown on chart.

Press finished stitchery facedown on a padded surface. Mat and frame as desired.

MATERIALS
FOR THE ROSE SHOE CLIPS

FABRIC
*Two 6×6-inch pieces of 28-count white linen
Two 3×3-inch pieces of lightweight fusible interfacing*

FLOSS
*Cotton embroidery floss in colors listed in key
1 additional skein of dark rose pink (DMC 961)*

SUPPLIES
*Needle; embroidery hoop
Two 1½-inch-diameter button forms
Wire cutters; 2 shoe clip findings; fine sandpaper
All-purpose cement; crafts glue*

INSTRUCTIONS
FOR THE ROSE SHOE CLIPS

Tape or zigzag fabric edges. Find center of chart and of fabric; begin stitching there. Use three plies of floss to work cross-stitches over two threads of fabric. Work backstitches using one ply.

Press linen on wrong side. Fuse interfacing to back of stitched pieces following manufacturer's instructions. Centering motif over button forms, trim fabric ½ inch beyond edge. Run a gathering thread ¼ inch from the cut edge. Pull thread to smooth linen around top of form.

Assemble the button back following manufacturer's instructions. Use wire cutters to remove button shanks. Sand center back of button and backs of shoe clips. Using cement, glue shoe clips to back of button forms.

For twisted cord, cut three 16-inch strands of the pink floss; combine into a single strand. Twist until entire strand is tightly wound; fold in half. Hold two ends while two halves twist around each other. Starting at bottom of one covered button form, glue twisted cord around covered button form for each shoe clip.

continued on page 46

MATERIALS
FOR THE RICE BAG

FABRIC

8×6-inch piece of 28-count white linen
½ yard of 45-inch-wide pink satin

FLOSS

Cotton embroidery floss in colors listed in key

SUPPLIES

Needle; embroidery hoop
Nine 2½-millimeter pearls
White sewing thread
½ yard of ⅛-inch-diameter cording
⅓ yard of ½-inch-wide white pregathered lace
1 yard each ⅛-inch-wide pink, green, and
lavender satin ribbons

INSTRUCTIONS
FOR THE RICE BAG

Tape or zigzag the edges of fabric to prevent fraying. Find center of chart and center of fabric; begin stitching there. Use three plies of floss to work cross-stitches over two threads of fabric. Work backstitches using one ply of floss. Use sewing thread to attach pearls. Press linen facedown on a padded surface.

Trim linen ½ inch beyond bottom row of stitches. Trim remaining sides to make a 3½×5¾-inch rectangle. From satin cut three 3½×5¾-inch rectangles, a ¾×14-inch bias piping strip, and a 1¾×22-inch bias ruffle strip. Sew seams with right sides together using ¼-inch seam allowances unless otherwise noted.

Center cording lengthwise on wrong side of piping strip. Fold fabric around cording, raw edges together. Use a zipper foot to sew through both layers close to cording. Pin covered cording to sides and bottom of linen bag front, raw edges even. Sew one satin rectangle (bag back) to linen bag front. Clip corners and turn right side out.

Baste lace to right side of bag top edge with straight edge of lace just inside ¼-inch seam allowances. Whipstitch lace ends together. Join short ends of ruffle strip; fold in half lengthwise with wrong sides together.

Sew a gathering thread through both layers ¼ inch from raw edges. Pull threads to fit top of bag, with raw edges even. Stitch, along basting, sandwiching lace between bag and ruffle.

For lining, sew long sides of remaining satin rectangles, right sides together. Do not turn. Slip bag into lining with right sides facing. Sew top of lining to top of bag; pull lining right side out. Turn under ¼ inch along bottom edges of lining; slipstitch closed. Tuck lining into bag. Knot ribbon ends and tie around bag.

MATERIALS
FOR THE HANDKERCHIEF

FABRIC

Purchased 10¾×10¾-inch linen handkerchief
with hemstitched edge
4×4-inch piece of 14-count waste canvas

FLOSS

Cotton embroidery floss in colors listed in key

SUPPLIES

Needle; basting thread
Five 2½-millimeter pearls
White sewing thread; tweezers
1¼ yard of ⅞-inch-wide white flat lace
1¾ yards of blue Ribbonfloss or
1/16-inch-wide ribbon

INSTRUCTIONS
FOR THE HANDKERCHIEF

Tape or zigzag the edges of waste canvas to prevent fraying. Baste waste canvas at a 45 degree angle over one handkerchief corner.

Measure 1½ inches from bottom edge of handkerchief; begin stitching lower edge of stem there. Use three plies of floss to work cross-stitches. Work backstitches using one ply of floss. Use sewing thread to attach pearls.

Use tweezers to carefully pull the waste canvas threads from under the cross-stitches. Press finished stitchery on wrong side. Sew lace around edges of handkerchief. Weave ribbon through hemstitched edge of handkerchief; tie ends into a bow.

RIBBON AND ROSES WEDDING		
ANCHOR	DMC	
002	⊡	000 White
118	✶	340 Medium periwinkle
117	⊞	341 Light periwinkle
253	⊙	471 Light avocado
878	⬤	501 Dark blue green
877	◣	502 Medium blue green
875	▢	503 True blue green
076	▲	961 Dark rose pink
075	▽	962 Medium rose pink
073	⊟	963 Pale rose pink
681	▼	3051 Dark gray green
025	✕	3716 Light rose pink
1030	◈	3746 Dark periwinkle
120	⊡	3747 Pale periwinkle
BACKSTITCH		
267	╱	469 Dark avocado– small and medium leaves, vine
683	╱	500 Deep blue green– large leaves
059	╱	600 Cranberry–roses
131	╱	798 Delft blue– small flowers
1030	╱	3746 Dark periwinkle– ribbon, lettering
STRAIGHT STITCH		
002	╱	000 White–border
PEARLS		
	●	White–border

HANKIE stitch count: 28 high x 17 wide
HANKIE finished design sizes:
14-count fabric – 2 x 1¼ inches
18-count fabric – 1½ x 1 inches

SHOE CLIP stitch count: 18 high x 19 wide
SHOE CLIP finished design sizes:
14-count fabric – 1¼ x 1⅜ inches
18-count fabric – 1 x 1 inches

RICE BAG stitch count: 41 high x 22 wide
RICE BAG finished design sizes:
14-count fabric – 2⅞ x 1½ inches
18-count fabric – 2¼ x 1¼ inches

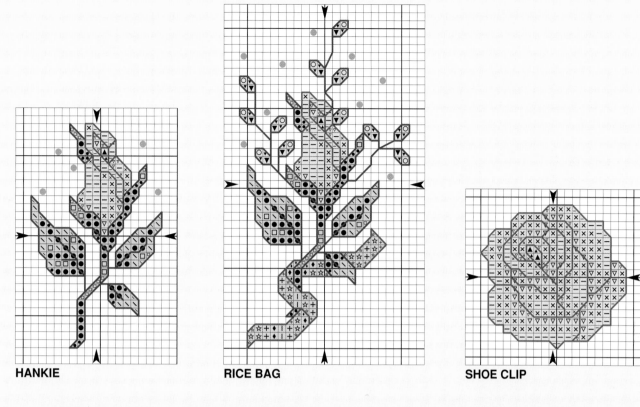

HANKIE

RICE BAG

SHOE CLIP

RIBBON AND ROSES WEDDING ALPHABET

RIBBON AND ROSES WEDDING SAMPLER

ANCHOR		DMC	
002	·	000	White
118	★	340	Medium periwinkle
117	+	341	Light periwinkle
267	✱	469	Dark avocado
266	△	470	Medium avocado
253	○	471	Light avocado
878	●	501	Dark blue green
877	╱	502	Medium blue green
875	□	503	True blue green
293	◇	727	Topaz
128	╲	775	Baby blue
076	◀	961	Dark rose pink
075	▷	962	Medium rose pink
073	│	963	Pale rose pink
681	▼	3051	Dark gray green
262	⊞	3052	Medium gray green

ANCHOR		DMC	
025	✕	3716	Light rose pink
1030	◆	3746	Dark periwinkle
120	▬	3747	Pale periwinkle

BACKSTITCH

267	╱	469	Dark avocado – small and medium leaves, vine
683	╱	500	Deep blue green – large leaves

ANCHOR		DMC	

BACKSTITCH

059	╱	600	Cranberry – roses
131	╱	798	Delft blue – small flowers
1030	╱	3746	Dark periwinkle – ribbon, lettering

STRAIGHT STITCH

002	╱	000	White – border

PEARLS

● White – border

WEDDING SAMPLER stitch count:
184 high x 143 wide
WEDDING SAMPLER
finished design sizes:
14-count fabric – 13⅛ x 10¼ inches
18-count fabric – 10¼ x 8 inches

Wedding Sampler

This elegant hardanger-and-cross-stitch sampler will be displayed forever to remember that wonderful day. Stitch this lovely piece on 22-count antique white hardanger fabric. For a finishing touch, add pearl beads and delicate silk-ribbon embroidery.

MATERIALS

FABRIC
18×22-inch piece of 22-count antique white hardanger fabric

FLOSS
Cotton embroidery floss and 4-mm silk ribbon in colors listed in key
#5 white pearl cotton

SUPPLIES
Needle
Embroidery hoop
Seed beads in color listed in key
Ecru floss
Desired mat and frame

INSTRUCTIONS

Tape or zigzag the edges of the fabric to prevent fraying. Measure 3¼ inches from center top of fabric; begin stitching center of top border there.

Use three plies of floss for cross-stitches and two plies of floss for Algerian eyelets (diagram is on *page 25*). Work the backstitches using one ply of floss. Work satin stitches and needleweaving, *page 55*, using one strand of pearl cotton. Work the ribbon embroidery stitches using one strand of silk ribbon. Attach the beads using one ply of ecru floss.

Press the finished stitchery from the back, avoiding the roses. Mat and frame the piece as desired.

WEDDING SAMPLER

ANCHOR	DMC	
074	⊟	3354 Light dusty rose
076	⬤	3731 Dark dusty rose
075	☒	3733 Medium dusty rose
140	⊞	3755 Baby blue

BACKSTITCH

132	/	797 Royal blue – lettering
045	/	814 Garnet – ribbon

ALGERIAN EYELET

390	✸	822 Beige-gray

BEADS

⬤	03021 Royal pearl Mill Hill Antique seed bead

SATIN STITCH
#5 White pearl cotton

NEEDLEWEAVING
#5 White pearl cotton

FRENCH KNOT RIBBON EMBROIDERY
Pale yellow silk ribbon

LAZY DAISY RIBBON EMBROIDERY
Light green silk ribbon

SPIDER WEB ROSES RIBBON EMBROIDERY
Two-toned rose silk ribbon

Stitch count: 171 high x 135 wide
Finished design sizes:
22-count fabric –15½ x 12¼ inches
25-count fabric –13⅝ x 10⅞ inches

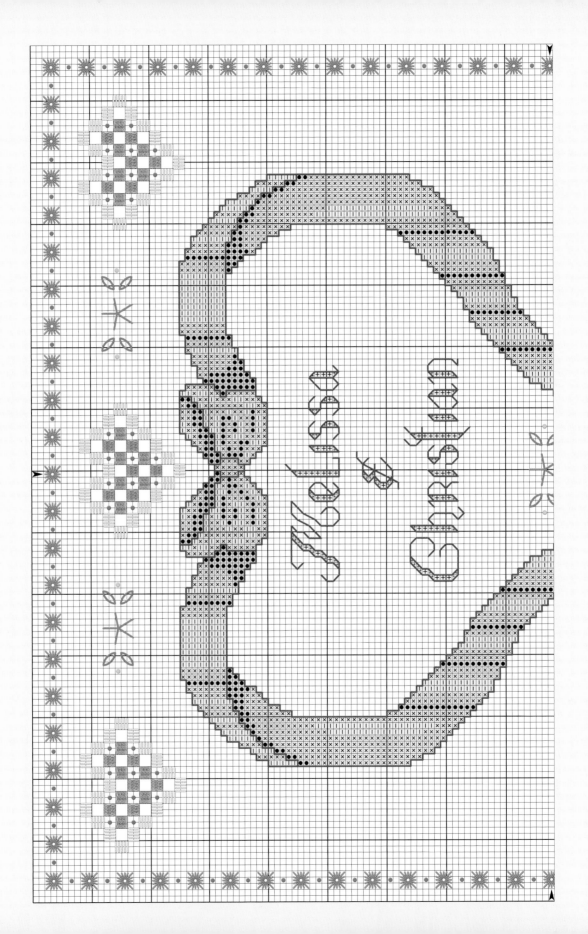

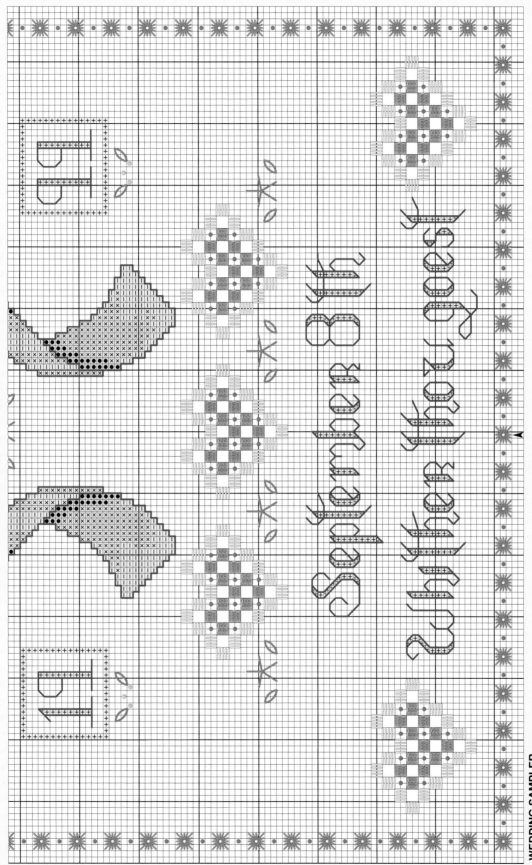

WEDDING SAMPLER

WEDDING SAMPLER ALPHABET

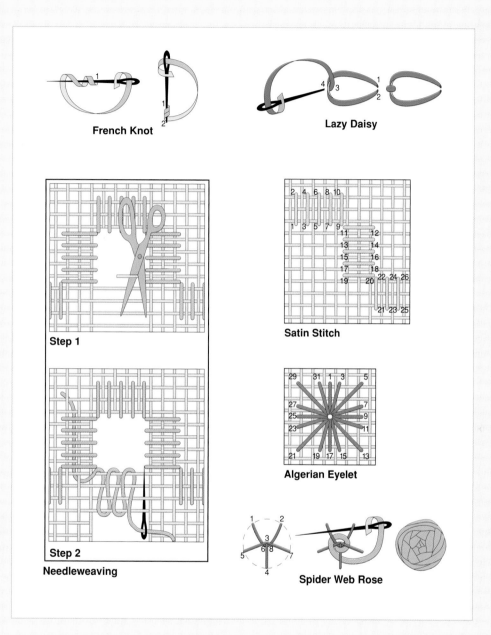

French Knot

Lazy Daisy

Step 1

Step 2

Needleweaving

Satin Stitch

Algerian Eyelet

Spider Web Rose

To Have & To Hold

Present a gift the happy couple will remember always by stitching one of these designs. Bride and groom cake-topper figurines are worked on 28-count Monaco fabric. Sew the shapes, stuff with fiberfill, and trim them with delicate braid. Stitch the lifelike roses on 14-count perforated paper. The charts begin on page 58, the key is on page 59.

MATERIALS

FABRIC (FOR BOTH FIGURES)
Four 9×7-inch pieces of 28-count white Monaco fabric

FLOSS (FOR BOTH FIGURES)
Cotton embroidery floss in colors listed in key
1 additional skein each of
Black (DMC 310)
Pale old gold (DMC 677)
Off-white (DMC 746)
Yellow (DMC 3823)

SUPPLIES (FOR EACH)
Needle; tracing paper; lightweight cardboard
Thick white crafts glue
7½-inch piece of white cording; sewing thread
Polyester fiberfill
8×8-inch piece of white cotton fabric
FOR GROOM
12-inch piece of black-and-gold braided trim
FOR BRIDE
12-inch piece of gold braided trim

INSTRUCTIONS

Tape or zigzag the edges of the fabric to prevent fraying. Find center of chart and of fabric; begin stitching there.

Use three plies of floss to work cross-stitches over two threads of fabric. Work petite stitches using one ply over one thread for the bride's head back, faces, lapel detail, and bridal bouquet. Work backstitches using one ply.

Trace the patterns, *page 59*, onto a folded piece of tracing paper. Cut out. Center tracing paper pattern over design, draw around shape, and cut out. Trace base pattern onto cardboard. Add ½ inch around edge and cut from white fabric. Cover the cardboard with the fabric; glue edges to back. Sew the front and back body pieces together, right sides facing, leaving bottom open. Turn right side out. Stuff firmly with fiberfill. Slipstitch the base to bottom of figure.

For the groom, glue black-and-gold trim around outer edges of figure. For the bride, glue gold trim around outside edges of figure.

Glue white cording around the bottoms of the bases.

Rose stitch count: 20 high x 25 wide
Rose finished design sizes:
14-count fabric – 1 3/8 x 1 3/4 inches
11-count fabric – 1 7/8 x 2 1/4 inches
18-count fabric – 1 1/8 x 1 3/8 inches

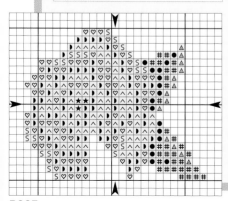

ROSE

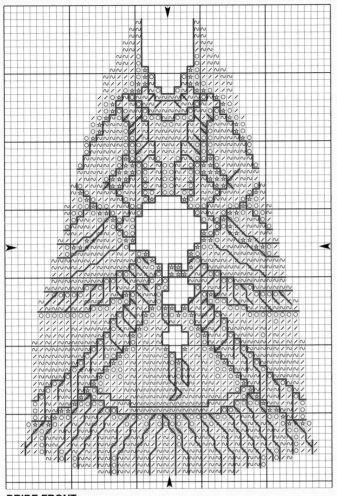

BRIDE FRONT

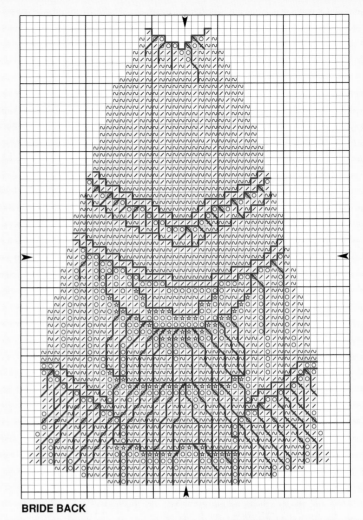

BRIDE BACK

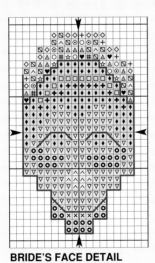

BRIDE'S FACE DETAIL

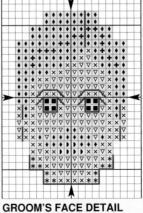

BRIDE'S HEAD BACK

**GROOM'S
LAPEL DETAIL**

Bride stitch count: 70 high x 20 wide
Bride finished design sizes:
14-count fabric – 5 x 3¹/₄ inches
11-count fabric – 6¹/₃ x 4¹/₈ inches
18-count fabric – 3⁷/₈ x 2¹/₂ inches

GROOM'S FACE DETAIL

Groom stitch count: 70 high x 20 wide
Groom finished design sizes:
14-count fabric – 5 x 1³/₈ inches
11-count fabric – 6¹/₃ x 1⁷/₈ inches
18-count fabric – 3⁷/₈ x 1¹/₈ inches

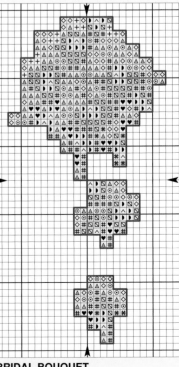

BRIDAL BOUQUET

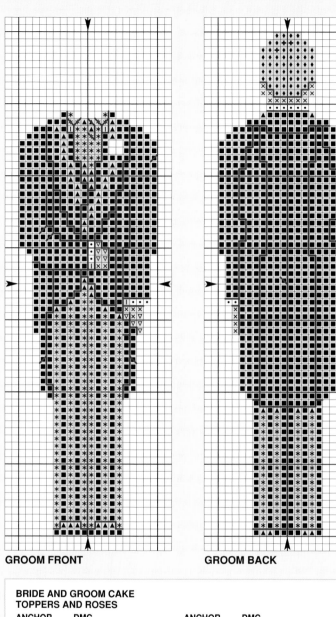

GROOM FRONT

GROOM BACK

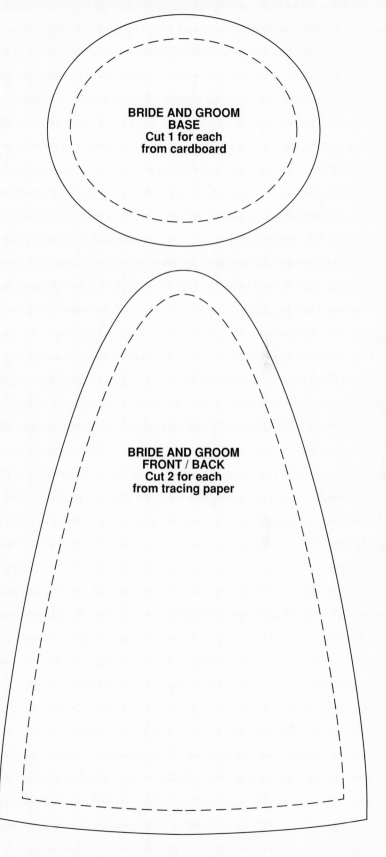

**BRIDE AND GROOM
BASE
Cut 1 for each
from cardboard**

**BRIDE AND GROOM
FRONT / BACK
Cut 2 for each
from tracing paper**

**BRIDE AND GROOM CAKE
TOPPERS AND ROSES**

ANCHOR		DMC	ANCHOR		DMC
002	·	000 White	891	☆	676 Light old gold
403	■	310 Black	886	○	677 Pale old gold
400	✳	317 True pewter	275	~	746 Off white
218	●	319 Dark pistachio	1012	×	754 Medium peach
215	△	320 True pistachio	234	I	762 Pearl gray
059	★	326 Deep rose	024	♡	776 Medium pink
038	⌃	335 Medium rose	136	♥	799 Medium Delft blue
008	⊙	353 Dark peach	144	+	800 Pale Delft blue
217	⊞	367 Medium pistachio	130	◎	809 True Delft blue
214	◇	368 Light pistachio	023	S	818 Pale pink
401	▲	413 Dark pewter	052	▶	899 Light rose
310	◆	434 Medium chestnut	1011	▽	948 Light peach
1046	✚	435 Dark chestnut	036	⊠	3326 Pale rose
1045	□	436 Tan	386	⁄	3823 Yellow

BACKSTITCH
392 ⁄ 642 Beige gray – all
back stitches

Dogwood Wedding Sampler

A gently curving spray of dogwood blossoms and a dainty hearts border and beads frame this sentimental poem— written by a mother on the occasion of her child's wedding. The sentiments are universal for parents on such a joyous day. Share your special feelings of love and pride with your son or daughter by stitching this beautiful wedding design. The chart is on pages 62–63.

MATERIALS

FABRIC
16×20-inch piece of 28-count white linen

FLOSS
Cotton embroidery floss in colors listed in key

SUPPLIES
Embroidery hoop
Needle
Seed beads in color listed in key
Graph paper; pencil
Desired mat and frame

DOGWOOD WEDDING SAMPLER

ANCHOR		DMC	
002	·	000	White
358	╱	433	Golden brown
359	■	801	Medium coffee brown
244	▲	987	Medium forest green
242	⊞	989	Pale forest green
068	◉	3687	True mauve
060	✕	3688	Medium mauve
049	⊟	3689	Light mauve

BEADS

	✳		Mill Hill seed bead 00145 pink

BACKSTITCH

360	╱	898	Dark coffee brown – leaves, veins, stems (1X)
1028	╱	3685	Dark mauve – flowers (1X), lettering (2X)

Stitch count: 198 high x 135 wide

Finished design sizes:
14-count fabric – 14⅛ x 9¾ inches
11-count fabric – 18 x 12⅜ inches
18-count fabric – 11 x 7½ inches

INSTRUCTIONS

Tape or zigzag edges of fabric to prevent fraying. Using one 16-inch edge of fabric as top, measure 5 inches from top and 3 inches from left edge; begin stitching square motif from upper left-hand corner of chart there.

Work all cross-stitches using two plies of floss over two threads of fabric. For beaded areas, work half cross-stitches; attach beads on return stitch as shown in diagram, *page 162*. Work backstitches as specified in key.

Chart desired names and date on graph paper using alphabet on *page 63*. Separate letters with one square.

Center and stitch charted names and date, positioning the top edge eight rows (16 threads) below last line of the poem. Press finished stitchery facedown and frame as desired.

On Your Wedding Day

We remember well the day
you came into our life;

The days of childish laughter,
the days of childish strife.

We remember the little hurts
we tried to kiss away;

And how we beamed so proudly
on graduation day.

Today you stand before us
repeating wedding vows

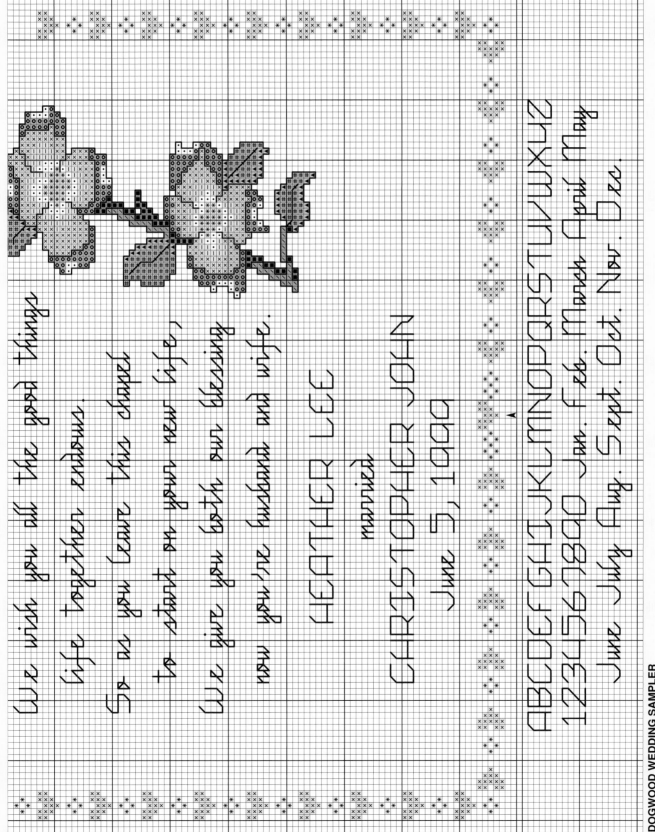

We wish you all the good things
life together endures.

So as you leave this chapel
to start on your new life,

We give you both our blessing
now you're husband and wife.

HEATHER LEE
married
CHRISTOPHER JOHN
June 5, 1999

ABCDEFGHIJKLMNOPQRSTUVWXYZ
1234567890 Jan. Feb. March April May
June July Aug. Sept. Oct. Nov. Dec.

DOGWOOD WEDDING SAMPLER

Friendship Sachet

Start a tradition by exchanging handmade gifts with friends. This tiny treasure of stitches can be given as a decorative ornament or as a lovely sachet.

MATERIALS

FABRIC
8×8-inch piece of 28-count white Jobelan fabric

FLOSS
Cotton embroidery floss in colors listed in key

SUPPLIES
Needle; embroidery hoop
8×8-inch piece of pink satin
Polyester fiberfill or scented potpourri sachet
23-inch piece of ½-inch-wide pink satin ribbon
8-inch piece of ¼-inch pink satin ribbon

INSTRUCTIONS

Tape or zigzag fabric edges. Find center of chart and of fabric; begin stitching there.

Use three plies of floss to work cross-stitches over two threads of fabric. Work backstitches using one ply.

Cut fabric into a heart shape as indicated on pattern. Using the stitchery as a pattern, cut a heart shape from the pink satin. Gather wide ribbon and sew to edge of heart front, tucking in a narrow ribbon loop at the top. Sew the pieces together with right sides facing using a ¼-inch seam allowance and leaving one side open. Turn, stuff with fiberfill or scented potpourri sachet, and handsew the opening closed.

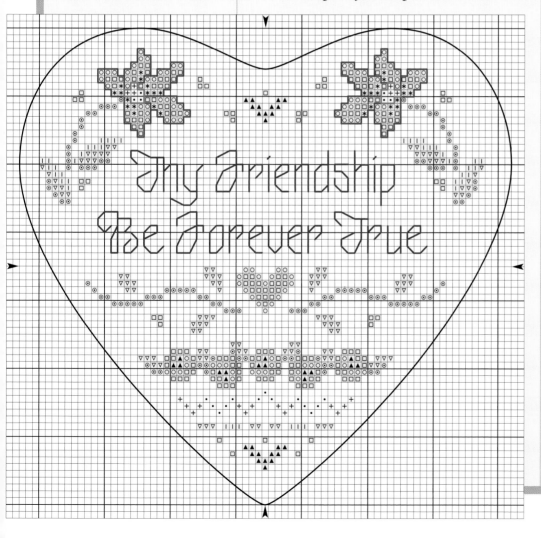

ANCHOR		DMC	
215	⊙	320	True pistachio
214	▽	368	Light pistachio
1043	I	369	Pale pistachio
891	+	676	Light old gold
886	•	677	Pale old gold
059	▲	3350	Deep dusty rose
074	□	3354	Light dusty rose
049	○	3689	Mauve
075	✱	3733	Medium dusty rose

BACKSTITCH

401	/	413 Pewter – lettering (1X)
901	/	680 Dark old gold – top flower centers (1X)
059	/	3350 Deep dusty rose – top flowers (1X)

Stitch count: 62 high x 68 wide

Finished design sizes:
14-count fabric – 4⅜ x 4⅞ inches
11-count fabric – 5⅝ x 6⅛ inches
16-count fabric – 3⅞ x 4¼ inches

Button Sampler

This delightful poem about family memories can be embellished with buttons from Grandma's collection or newly purchased ones. Worked on linen in soft muted shades, the design has the look of an antique piece; stitched on Aida cloth in primary colors, the effect is crisp and contemporary. This charming design, custom-made for your family, is sure to tug at the heartstrings of old and young alike. The chart and key are on pages 68–69.

MATERIALS

FABRIC
24×18-inch piece of 25-count driftwood Dublin linen fabric or 14-count ivory Aida cloth

FLOSS
Cotton embroidery floss in colors listed in key

SUPPLIES
Embroidery hoop; needle
18 buttons in assorted colors and sizes
Desired frame and mat

INSTRUCTIONS

Tape or zigzag edges of fabric to prevent fraying. Find center of chart and center of fabric; begin stitching there.

Work cross-stitches using two plies of floss. Backstitch title, Family Buttons, using two plies of floss. Work all other backstitches using one ply of floss. For linen, work all stitches over two threads of fabric, except work dots over lowercase i's over one thread. For Aida cloth, work dots over lowercase i's as French knots.

Press the finished stitchery on the reverse side. Sew buttons over cross-stitched buttons of sampler. Frame as desired.

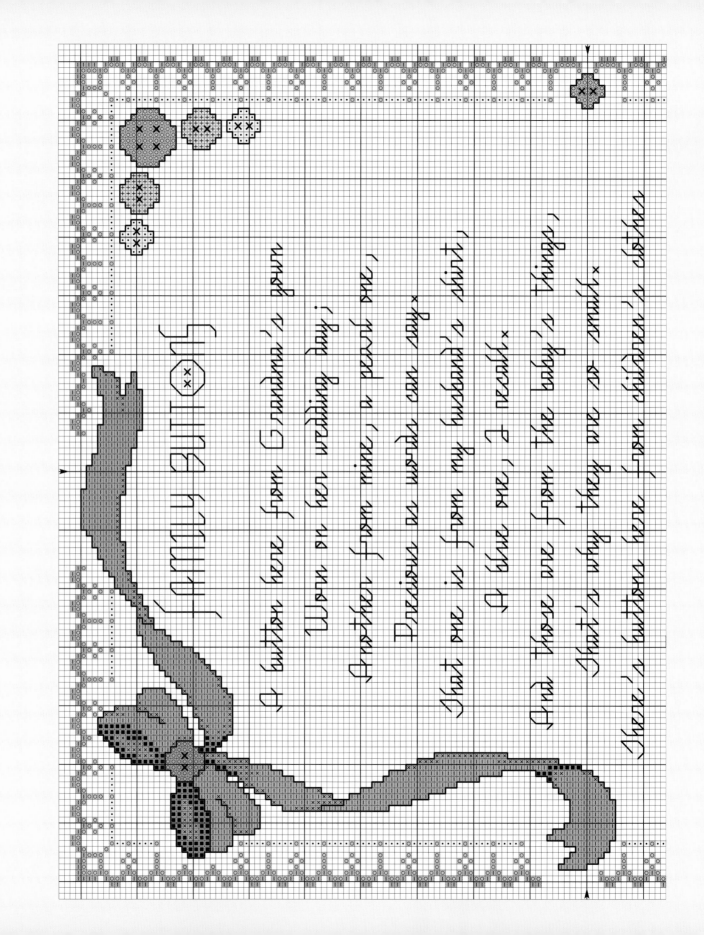

FAMILY BUTTONS

A button here from Grandma's gown

Worn on her wedding day;

Another from mine, a pearl one,

Precious no words can say.

That one is from my husband's shirt,

A blue one, I recall.

And these are from the baby's things,

That's why they are so small.

There's buttons here from children's clothes

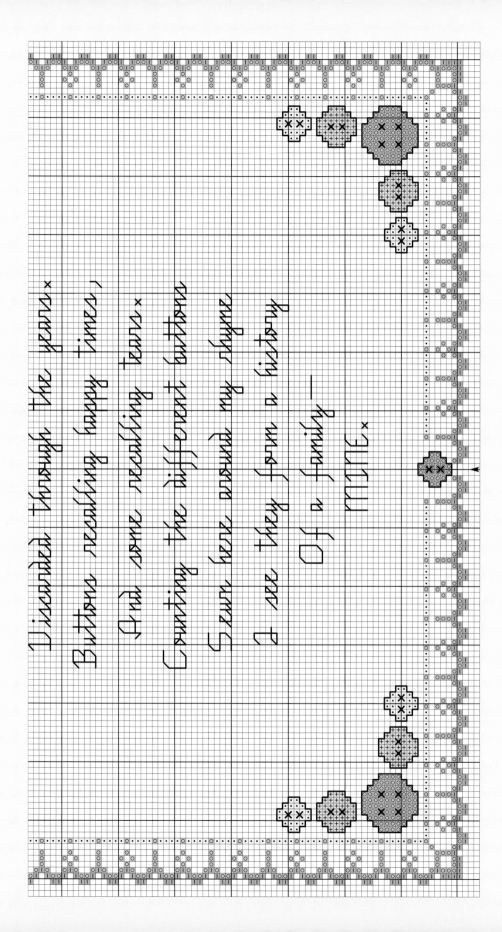

Discarded through the years,
Buttons recalling happy times,
And some recalling tears.
Counting the different buttons
Sewn here around my rhyme,
I see they form a history—
Of a family—
MINE.

BUTTON SAMPLER–Neutral colors

ANCHOR	DMC		ANCHOR	DMC
926	•	712 Cream	899	◎ 3782 Light brown
851	■	924 Dark blue		**BACKSTITCH**
850	✕	926 Medium blue	1050	╱ 3781 Dark brown–
848	I	927 Light blue		lettering, ribbon,
274	✛	928 Gray		and buttons

BUTTON SAMPLER–Primary colors

ANCHOR	DMC		ANCHOR	DMC
290	•	444 Canary	013	✛ 817 Nasturtium
1005	✕	498 Dark red		**BACKSTITCH**
046	I	666 Medium red	152	╱ 823 Navy–lettering,
131	◎	798 Blue		ribbon, and
045	■	814 Garnet		buttons

Stitch count: 184 high x 142 wide
Finished design sizes:
28-count fabric – 13 1/8 x 10 1/8 inches
25-count fabric – 14 3/4 x 11 3/8 inches
36-count fabric – 10 1/4 x 7 7/8 inches

Beautiful
Florals

The universal language of flowers is captured in all its glory in this spring-fresh chapter. You'll find old-fashioned pansies, elegant roses, variegated lilies, and other joyful blooms to inspire your next project. Whether these colorful cross-stitched motifs are framed, sewn into pillows, set into serving trays, or made into jewelry, each is a treasure that shares the beauty of our world.

A collage of sweet bouquets adorn this springtime sampler. Tiny lazy daisy flowers add a delicate touch to the colorful display.

Elegant Blooms Sampler

MATERIALS

FABRIC
14×14-inch piece of 28-count white Lugana fabric

THREADS
Cotton embroidery floss in colors listed in key

SUPPLIES
Needle; embroidery hoop; desired mat and frame

INSTRUCTIONS

Tape or zigzag fabric edges. Find center of chart and of fabric; begin stitching there. Use three plies of floss to work cross-stitches over two threads of fabric. Work backstitches using one ply. Press stitchery from the back. Mat and frame as desired.

ANCHOR		DMC
110	▲	208 Dark lavender
108	◯	210 Light lavender
342	Ⅰ	211 Pale lavender
893	∕	224 Shell pink
256	⟍	704 Chartreuse
305	✳	725 True topaz
295	▽	726 Light topaz
293	−	727 Pale topaz
304	#	741 Tangerine
024	⋀	776 Medium pink
027	✶	899 Light rose
244	⋀	987 Medium forest green
242	✕	989 Pale forest green
292	•	3078 Lemon
059	⊙	3350 Dusty rose
087	◆	3607 Dark fuchsia
086	+	3608 Medium fuchsia
085	⊓	3609 Light fuchsia
875	‖	3813 Light blue-green
891	∼	3822 Light straw
176	+	3839 Lavender-blue
305	◲	3852 Deep straw

BACKSTITCH (1X)

1041	∕	844 Beaver gray – all stitches

STRAIGHT STITCH (1X)

256	∕	704 Chartreuse – lilies and center lavender flowers
292	∕	3078 Lemon – lilies

LAZY DAISY (1X)

110	⟋	208 Dark lavender – center flowers
256	⟋	704 Chartreuse – center lavender flower leaves
292	⟋	3078 Lemon – daffodils

Stitch count: 100 high x 100 wide
Finished design sizes:
28-count fabric – 7⅛ x 7⅛ inches
32-count fabric – 6¼ x 6¼ inches
36-count fabric – 5½ x 5½ inches

In the Garden

Mother Nature's finest are colorfully displayed in this beautiful framed piece. Blooms and birdhouses, butterflies and birds turn an ordinary garden into a backyard sanctuary. Stitched on 28-count denim blue Jobelan fabric using vibrant colors, this keepsake will bring a breath of fresh air into a room in spring or anytime of the year. The chart is on pages 76–77.

MATERIALS

FABRIC
19×14-inch piece of 28-count denim blue Jobelan fabric

FLOSS
Cotton embroidery floss in colors listed in key

SUPPLIES
Needle
Embroidery hoop
Desired mat and frame

INSTRUCTIONS

Tape or zigzag fabric edges. Find center of chart and of fabric; begin stitching there.

Use three plies of floss to work cross-stitches over two threads of fabric. Work backstitches using one ply. Press and frame as desired.

Stitch count: 180 high x 136 wide
Finished design sizes:
11-count fabric – $16\frac{1}{2}$ x $12\frac{1}{2}$ inches
14-count fabric – 13 x $9\frac{3}{4}$ inches
18-count fabric – 10 x $7\frac{2}{3}$ inches

IN THE GARDEN SAMPLER

ANCHOR		DMC	
002	•	000	White
108	◎	210	Light lavender
342	◥	211	Pale lavender
403	■	310	Black
100	★	327	Antique violet
011	⊙	350	Medium coral
009	△	352	Pale coral
008	❘	353	Peach
233	▲	451	Shell gray
683	◆	500	Blue green
860	◑	522	Olive drab
099	▢	552	Violet
891	♡	676	Light old gold
901	▶	680	Dark old gold
226	▽	702	Christmas green
295	✳	726	Light topaz
293	+	727	Pale topaz
890	✕	729	Medium old gold
175	▣	794	Cornflower blue
045	⊠	814	Garnet
013	◤	817	Deep coral
134	◉	820	Royal blue
277	◢	831	Bronze
1041	♥	844	Beaver gray
340	◩	920	Copper
332	◍	946	Burnt orange
186	∧	959	Aqua
076	◀	961	Rose pink

ANCHOR		DMC	
314	⫴	970	Pumpkin
246	⊞	986	Forest green
905	⊠	3021	Brown gray
267	▬	3346	Hunter green
264	★	3348	Yellow green
262	◈	3363	Loden
382	●	3371	Black brown
1028	✚	3685	Deep mauve
049	◇	3689	Light mauve
1030	◆	3746	Dark periwinkle
120	☆	3747	Pale periwinkle
167	▭	3766	Peacock blue
1050	◉	3781	Mocha

STRAIGHT STITCH

403	╱	310 Black–butterfly antennae (2X)
226	╱	702 Christmas green–lilies (1X)
1028	╱	3685 Deep mauve–flowers on right side (1X)

BACKSTITCH

403	╱	310 Black–orange and blue butterflies (1X)
382	╱	3371 Black brown–all remaining stitches (1X)

FRENCH KNOT

403	✕	310 Black–butterfly antennae (1X)
226	✕	702 Christmas green–butterfly (1X)
293	✕	727 Pale topaz–flowers (1X)
134	✕	820 Royal blue–blue butterfly (1X)
332	✕	946 Burnt orange–butterfly (1X)
382	✕	3371 Black brown–butterfly and orange flowers at bottom (1X)

IN THE GARDEN SAMPLER

Consider the Lilies

Four splendid lilies, each a unique variety, surround the central alphabet in this elegant Easter sampler. The delicate colors in the petals, combined with the straight stitches and bullion knots of the stamens, give the lilies a fresh-from-the-garden look. Diagonal cross filling and other specialty stitches give lovely dimension to the graceful design. The chart and key are on pages 80–81.

MATERIALS

FABRIC
20×16-inch piece of 28-count bone Jobelan fabric

FLOSS
Cotton embroidery floss in colors listed in key on page 81
Pearl cotton in color listed in key on page 81

SUPPLIES
Needle; embroidery hoop

INSTRUCTIONS

Tape or zigzag edges of fabric. Find center of chart and center of fabric; begin stitching there.

Use three plies of floss to work cross-stitches over two threads of fabric before working specialty stitches. Work backstitches using one ply unless otherwise specified in key.

Work straight stitches, bullion knots, rice stitches, diamond eyelet stitches, and diagonal cross filling stitches using floss or pearl cotton as specified in key and referring to the diagrams, *below.* For diamond eyelets, give each stitch a gentle tug to open a small hole. Press finished stitchery from the back and frame as desired.

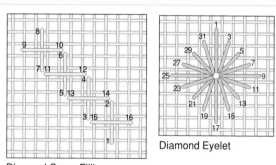

Diagonal Cross Filling

Diamond Eyelet

Rice Stitch

Bullion Knot

Stitch count: 192 high x 138 wide
Finished design sizes:
14-count fabric – 13¾ x 9⅞ inches
16-count fabric – 12 x 8⅝ inches
12½-count fabric – 15⅜ x 11 inches

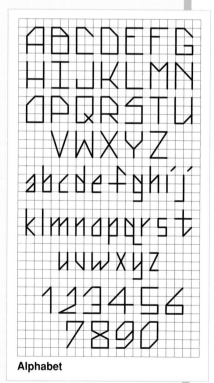

Alphabet

CONSIDER THE LILIES SAMPLER

ANCHOR		DMC	
002	•	000	White
979	■	312	Navy
977	✕	334	Dark baby blue
038	◈	335	Rose
1025	◉	347	Salmon
011	✱	350	Medium coral
009	□	920	Copper
008	▥	353	Pale coral
217	◉	367	Pistachio
398	◆	415	Light pearl gray
373	★	422	Hazel
266	◭	471	Avocado
273	◆	645	Dark beaver gray
1040	#	647	True beaver gray
295	╱	726	Topaz
316	☆	740	Dark tangerine
303	▽	742	Light tangerine

ANCHOR		DMC	
275	⁄	746	Off white
234	+	762	Pale pearl gray
128	—	775	Light baby blue
045	◢	814	Dark garnet
043	▶	815	Medium garnet
1044	⊕	895	Hunter green
340	⊙	920	Copper
1033	◇	932	Antique blue
355	▨	975	Golden brown
242	‖	989	Forest green
049	−	3689	Mauve
025	○	3716	Rose pink

BACKSTITCH

979	╱	312	Navy–alphabet flourish (2X), alphabet outline (1X)

BACKSTITCH

ANCHOR		DMC	
043	╱	815	Medium garnet–pistil end and center lines on pink lily in lower left corner (2X)
1033	╱	932	Antique blue–centers of white lily petals in upper left corner (2X)
381	╱	938	Coffee brown–all remaining stitches

STRAIGHT STITCH

217	╱	367	Pistachio–stamens and pistils (2X)
043	╱	815	Medium garnet–spots on pink lily petals in lower left corner (1X)
340	╱	920	Copper–spots on white lily petals in upper right corner (1X)

BULLION KNOT

ANCHOR		DMC	
303	—	742	Light tangerine–white lily stamen ends in upper left corner (2X)
043	●	815	Medium garnet–white lily stamen ends in lower left corner (2X)
340	●	920	Copper–white lily stamen ends in upper right corner (2X)
381	—	938	Coffee brown–coral lily stamen ends in lower right corner (2X)

RICE STITCH

303	⊠	742	Light tangerine–bottom (2X)
275	⊠	746	Off white–top (2X)

DIAMOND EYELET STITCH

355	✳	975	Golden brown (2X)

DIAGONAL CROSS FILLING

387	✢		Ecru #8 pearl cotton (1X)

The Flower Shop

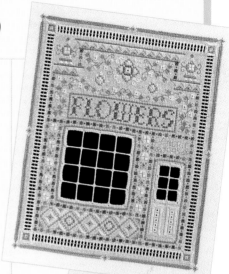

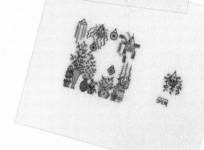

The beauty of garden flowers is everlasting in this collection of romantic designs. The exquisite flower shop is worked on two layers of fabric. The elaborately stitched lines of the exterior have Victorian charm, created with carefully placed specialty stitches. Colorful cross-stitched flowers and lush hanging plants, worked over one thread on the bottom layer, peek through the door and window. The charts, keys, and stitch diagrams begin on page 84.

MATERIALS

FABRIC
Two 16×14-inch pieces of 28-count ivory Jobelan fabric

FLOSS
Cotton embroidery floss in colors listed in key on page 87
Overdyed floss in color listed in key on page 87
#8 pearl cotton in color listed in key on page 87
#12 pearl cotton in colors listed in key on page 87

SUPPLIES
Needle; embroidery hoop
Graph paper; pencil
Desired frame and mat

INSTRUCTIONS

Tape or zigzag edges of each piece of Jobelan fabric to prevent fraying. For shop exterior, find vertical center of one piece of fabric. Measure 3½ inches from top of fabric; begin stitching diamond-shape motif as indicated by arrow on chart.

Work cross-stitches in each area, using two plies of floss over two threads, before working specialty stitches. Chart desired name and date using alphabet, *page 85*. Work backstitches using one ply of floss or one strand of pearl cotton. Use two plies of floss or one strand of pearl cotton to work satin stitches, upright cross-stitches, oblong cross-stitches, rice stitches, queen stitches (diagrams *page 84*), long-armed cross-stitches (see *page 94*), Smyrna cross-stitches, Algerian eyelets, diamond eyelets (see *page 25*), half diamond eyelets, and quarter diamond eyelets. For eyelets, give each stitch a gentle tug to open a hole in center.

Work border and windows last. At each corner of border, carefully clip eight threads close to satin stitches and remove. Use a 24-inch length of pearl cotton to work outer edge in serpentine stitches.

Anchor tails and carry threads inside satin stitches. Use a second 24-inch length of pearl cotton to work inner edge. Use a 24-inch length of pearl cotton for twisted ladder stitch.

For windows, after working satin stitch borders, carefully cut and remove threads indicated on chart. Use a 30-inch length of pearl cotton

continued on page 84

to work wrapped bars around remaining threads.

For the shop interior, find the vertical center of chart and the vertical center of the second piece of Jobelan. Measure 5½ inches from bottom of fabric; begin stitching center of the bottom row of chart there. Use one ply of floss to work the cross-stitches over one thread of fabric. Work backstitches using one ply. Use one ply to work star stitches, diamond eyelets, satin stitches, and Algerian eyelets. For eyelets, give each stitch a gentle tug to open a hole in center.

Press both pieces from the back. Position exterior on the interior so plants and sign appear through window openings; baste at sides of fabric to hold in place. Frame as desired.

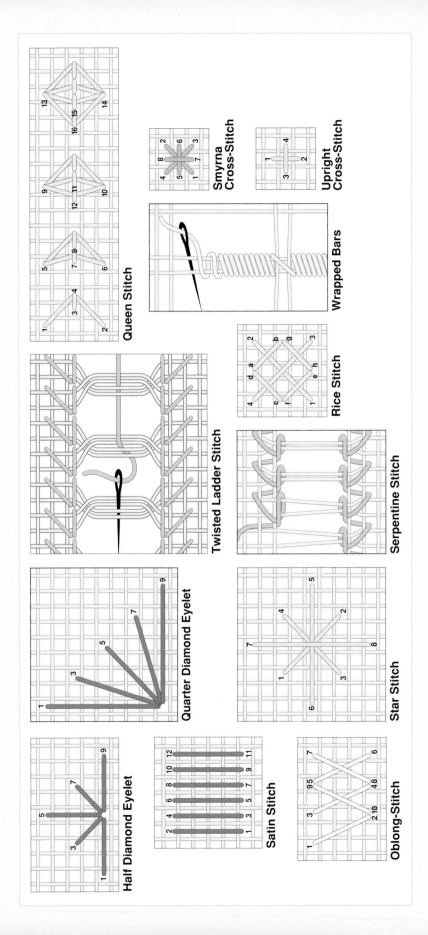

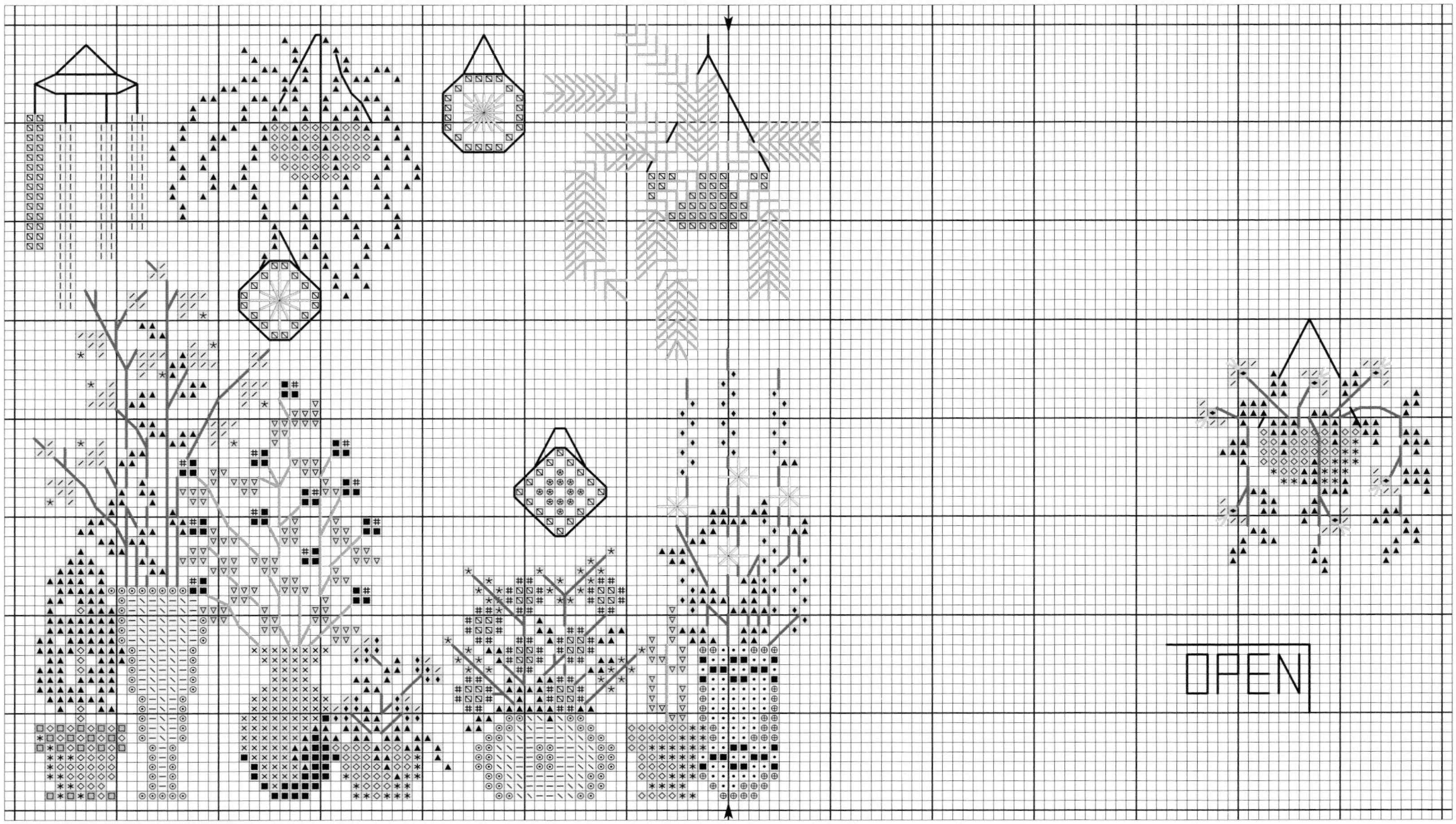

OPEN

FLOWER SHOP INTERIOR

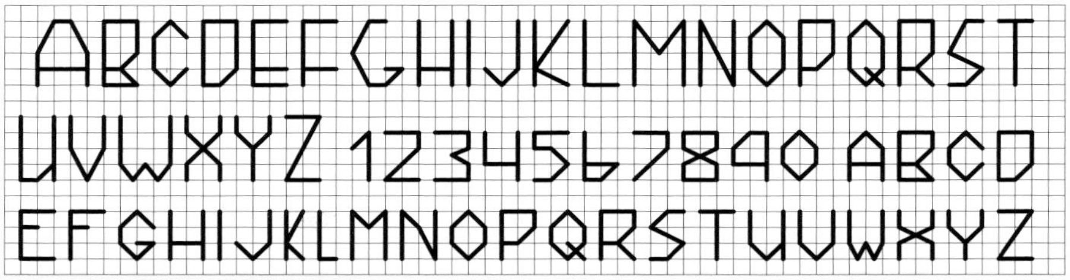

ABCDEFGHIJKLMNOPQRST
UVWXYZ 1234567890 ABCD
EFGHIJKLMNOPQRSTUVWXYZ

FLOWER SHOP ALPHABET

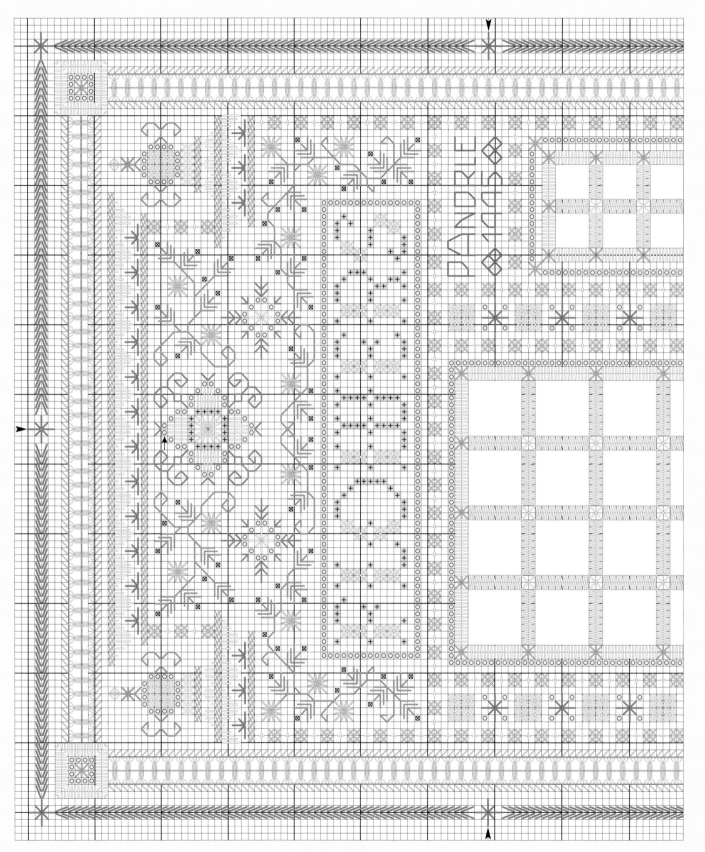

FLOWER SHOP EXTERIOR

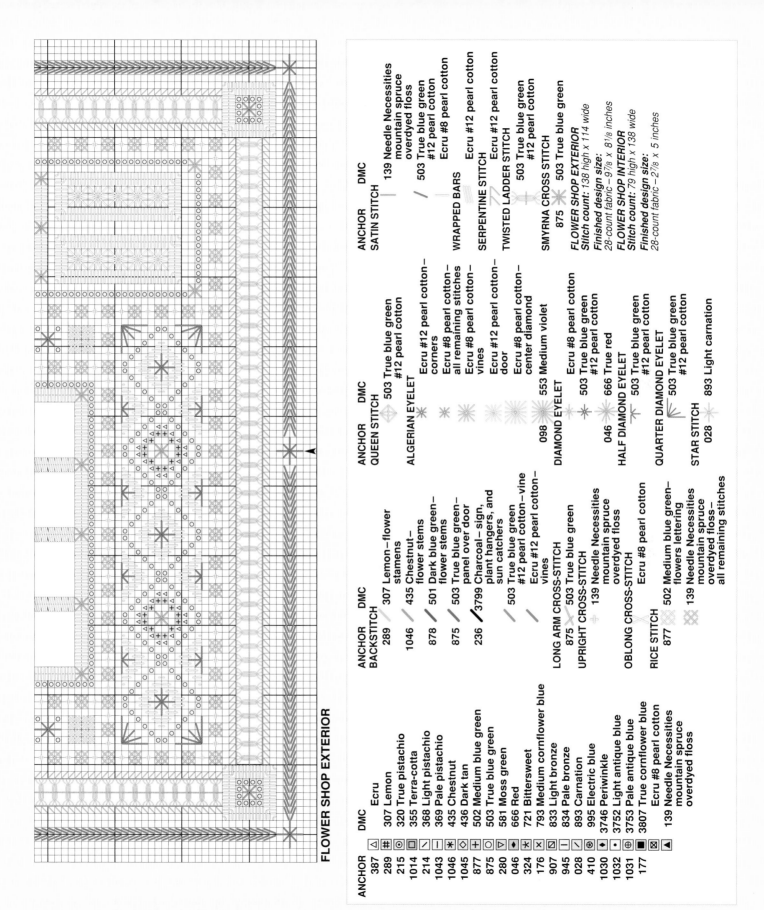

ANCHOR — DMC

ANCHOR	DMC	
387		Ecru
289	307	Lemon
215	320	True pistachio
1014	355	Terra-cotta
214	368	Light pistachio
1043	369	Pale pistachio
1045	435	Chestnut
	436	Dark tan
877	502	Medium blue green
875	503	True blue green
280	581	Moss green
046	666	Red
324	721	Bittersweet
176	793	Medium cornflower blue
907	833	Light bronze
945	834	Pale bronze
028	893	Carnation
410	995	Electric blue
1030	3746	Periwinkle
1032	3752	Light antique blue
1031	3753	Pale antique blue
177	3807	True cornflower blue
		Ecru #8 pearl cotton
		139 Needle Necessities mountain spruce overdyed floss

BACKSTITCH

ANCHOR	DMC	
289	307	Lemon—flower stamens
1046	435	Chestnut—flower stems
878	501	Dark blue green—flower stems
875	503	True blue green—panel over door
236	3799	Charcoal—sign, plant hangers, and sun catchers
	503	True blue green #12 pearl cotton—vine
		Ecru #12 pearl cotton—vines

LONG ARM CROSS-STITCH

875	503	True blue green

UPRIGHT CROSS-STITCH

139 Needle Necessities mountain spruce overdyed floss

OBLONG CROSS-STITCH

Ecru #8 pearl cotton

RICE STITCH

877	502	Medium blue green—flowers lettering
		139 Needle Necessities mountain spruce overdyed floss—all remaining stitches

QUEEN STITCH

ANCHOR	DMC	
	503	True blue green #12 pearl cotton

ALGERIAN EYELET

		Ecru #12 pearl cotton—corners
		Ecru #8 pearl cotton—all remaining stitches
		Ecru #8 pearl cotton—vines
		Ecru #12 pearl cotton—door
		Ecru #8 pearl cotton—center diamond
098	553	Medium violet

DIAMOND EYELET

		Ecru #8 pearl cotton
	503	True blue green #12 pearl cotton
046	666	True red

HALF DIAMOND EYELET

	503	True blue green #12 pearl cotton

QUARTER DIAMOND EYELET

	503	True blue green #12 pearl cotton

STAR STITCH

028	893	Light carnation

SATIN STITCH

ANCHOR	DMC	
		139 Needle Necessities mountain spruce overdyed floss
	503	True blue green #12 pearl cotton
		Ecru #8 pearl cotton
		Ecru #12 pearl cotton

WRAPPED BARS

Ecru #12 pearl cotton

SERPENTINE STITCH

Ecru #12 pearl cotton

TWISTED LADDER STITCH

503 True blue green #12 pearl cotton

SMYRNA CROSS STITCH

875	503	True blue green

FLOWER SHOP EXTERIOR
Stitch count: 138 high x 114 wide
Finished design size:
28-count fabric—9⅞ x 8⅛ inches

FLOWER SHOP INTERIOR
Stitch count: 79 high x 138 wide
Finished design size:
28-count fabric—2⅞ x 5 inches

Old-Fashioned Pansies

The delicate charm of dainty pansies takes center stage in this quaint design. Display your finished stitchery in a rich wooden tray that is perfect for a dresser top or as a tea tray. Or send thoughts of love to a special friend by selecting a single pansy motif to stitch on button covers. The charts and key are on pages 90–91.

MATERIALS
FOR THE PANSY TRAY

FABRIC
13×16-inch piece of 28-count ivory Jobelan fabric

FLOSS
Cotton embroidery floss in colors listed in key on page 90

SUPPLIES
Needle; embroidery hoop
Purchased 9¾×12¾-inch wood tray
8⅜×11½-inch piece of self-stick mounting board with foam
Masking tape

INSTRUCTIONS
FOR THE PANSY TRAY

Tape or zigzag edges of fabric to prevent fraying. Measure 6 inches from the 13-inch edge and 4 inches from the 16-inch edge on one corner of the fabric; begin stitching the bottom row of the corner pansy leaf, as indicated by an arrow, there.

Use three plies of floss to work cross-stitches over two threads of the fabric. Use three plies of floss to work straight stitches. Work French knots using two plies of floss. When stitching is complete on the first corner, turn the fabric 180 degrees and stitch the opposite corner in the same manner. Press the finished stitchery from the back.

Peel the protective paper from the mounting board. Position the back of the fabric on the foam side of the mounting board and press to stick. Fold the excess fabric to the back and secure with masking tape. Assemble the tray following the manufacturer's instructions.

MATERIALS
FOR THE PANSY BUTTON COVERS

FABRIC
6×6-inch piece of 28-count ivory Jobelan fabric
3×3-inch piece of lightweight fusible interfacing

FLOSS
Cotton embroidery floss in colors listed in key

SUPPLIES
Needle; embroidery hoop
1-inch-diameter button form
Sewing thread; wire cutters
4½-inch piece of pink rattail cord
Crafts glue; button cover finding
All-purpose cement

continued on page 90

INSTRUCTIONS
FOR THE PANSY
BUTTON COVERS

Tape or zigzag edges of fabric to prevent fraying. Find center of desired pansy on chart and center of fabric; begin stitching there. Use two plies of floss to work cross-stitches over one thread of fabric. Work straight stitches using one ply. Work French knots using one ply.

Fuse interfacing to back of fabric following manufacturer's instructions. Center design over button form; trim fabric ½ inch beyond edge. Run gathering thread ¼ inch from cut edge; tighten gathers. Assemble button following the manufacturer's instructions. Remove button shank using wire cutters. Position cord around front of button cover, overlapping ends at bottom; glue raw ends to back. Cement the button to button cover finding.

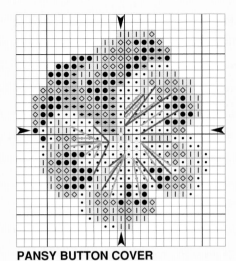

PANSY BUTTON COVER

PANSY TRAY AND BUTTON COVERS

ANCHOR		DMC	
042	●	309	Dark rose
979	■	312	Navy
977	⊙	334	Baby blue
267	◉	470	Medium avocado
266	▢	471	Light avocado
253	＋	472	Pale avocado
144	▬	800	Delft blue
161	✳	813	Powder blue
1005	◆	816	Garnet
161	◆	826	Bright blue
075			962	Rose pink
036	·	3326	Pale rose
076	◈	3731	Dusty rose

STRAIGHT STITCH

119	╱	333	Deep periwinkle–pink pansies

ANCHOR	DMC	
STRAIGHT STITCH		
118 ╱	340	Medium periwinkle–pink pansies
102 ╱	550	Deep violet–blue pansies
099 ╱	552	Dark violet–blue pansies
FRENCH KNOT		
300	745	Yellow–pansy centers

PANSY TRAY stitch count: 105 high x 151 wide
PANSY TRAY finished design sizes:
14-count fabric – 7½ x 10⅞ inches
11-count fabric – 9½ x 13¾ inches
16-count fabric – 6⅝ x 9⅜ inches

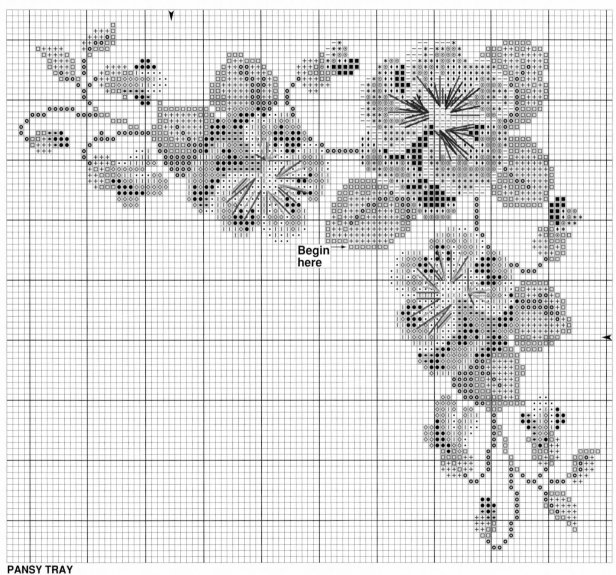

**Begin
here**

PANSY TRAY

Love One Another

These glorious designs, adapted from the antique print shown in the background, will surely be treasured throughout the years. Stitched on black Brittney fabric, the exquisite roses and sweet "Love One Another" sentiment are dramatic and romantic. The lovely set includes the timeless framed saying, a teapot cozy, and napkins. Charts, key, stitch diagrams, and teapot cozy pattern are on pages 94–99.

MATERIALS
FOR THE SAMPLER

FABRIC
18×27-inch piece of 28-count black Brittney fabric

FLOSS
*Cotton embroidery floss in colors listed in key
on* page 95
Pearl cotton as listed in key on page 95

SUPPLIES
Embroidery hoop; needle; desired mat and frame

INSTRUCTIONS
FOR THE SAMPLER

Tape or zigzag fabric edges. Find center of chart and center of fabric; begin stitching there.

Use three plies of floss to work cross-stitches over two threads of fabric. Work backstitches using two plies of floss unless otherwise specified in key. Work satin stitches with one strand of #3 pearl cotton. Use one strand of #12 pearl cotton to work long-armed cross variation, couching, and French knots. Press finished piece from the back and frame as desired.

MATERIALS
FOR THE TEA COZY

FABRIC
*10×12-inch piece of 28-count black Brittney fabric
10×12-inch piece of black fusible interfacing
Two 9×12-inch pieces of medium-weight fleece
½ yard of 45-inch-wide rose chintz*

FLOSS
*Cotton embroidery floss in colors listed in key
Pearl cotton as listed in key*

SUPPLIES
*Embroidery hoop; needle
¾ yard of ½-inch-wide black picot-edged lace
⅔ yard of purchased narrow black piping
Black and rose sewing threads; graph paper; pencil*

INSTRUCTIONS
FOR THE TEA COZY

Tape or zigzag edges of Brittney fabric to prevent fraying. Find center of chart and center of fabric; begin stitching there.

Use three plies of floss to work cross-stitches over two threads of fabric. Work backstitches using two plies of floss unless otherwise specified in key. Use one strand of #3 pearl cotton to work satin stitches. Use one strand of #12 pearl cotton to work long-armed cross variation, couching, and French knots. Fuse black interfacing to back of stitched fabric.

Enlarge the tea cozy pattern, *page 94,* using graph paper; cut out. For the front, center the pattern on the stitched area on wrong side of Brittney and trace; cut out. Use pattern to cut two interlining pieces from fleece and one back and two lining pieces from chintz. Also cut one 4×44-inch ruffle strip and one 1×4-inch loop from chintz. Pattern and measurements include ½-inch seam allowance.

Baste fleece interlinings to the wrong side of the Brittney front and the chintz back. On chintz back only, measure and

continued on page 94

mark a diagonal grid at 1½-inch intervals. Machine-quilt along marked lines using black thread. Baste straight edge of lace and raw edge of piping ¼ inch from rounded edge of Brittney front.

Fold ruffle strip in half lengthwise with raw edges even and wrong sides facing. Sew a gathering thread ½ inch from raw edges through both layers. Pull threads to fit rounded edge of front with raw edges even; adjust gathers evenly. Sew ruffle to cozy front along gathering line.

Fold 1×4-inch loop in half lengthwise. Turn raw edges in ¼ inch; topstitch. Fold loop in half crosswise, and pin raw edges at top center of front. Sew front to back with right sides facing, using ½-inch seams. Leave bottom open. Sew piping around bottom straight edge of tea cozy with raw edges even; set aside.

Sew lining pieces together with right sides facing, using ½ inch seams. Leave bottom open and an opening to turn at top. With right sides together, stitch cozy and lining together at bottom edge; turn. Slip-stitch opening closed. Tuck lining into cozy; press carefully.

MATERIALS
FOR THE NAPKIN

FABRIC
16¼×16¼-inch piece of 28-count black Brittney fabric

FLOSS
Cotton embroidery floss in colors listed in key
Pearl cotton as listed in key

SUPPLIES
1⅞ yards of ½-inch-wide black picot-edged lace

INSTRUCTIONS
FOR THE NAPKIN

Zigzag or serge edges of fabric to prevent fraying. Measure 1¼ inches from each edge at one corner of napkin; begin stitching the lower center of the small heart motif below the rose motif there.

Use three plies of floss to work cross-stitches over two threads of fabric. Work backstitches using two plies of floss unless otherwise specified in key. Use one strand of #12 pearl cotton to work long-armed cross variation, couching, and French knots.

Fold zigzagged edges under ¼ inch, mitering corners, and topstitch in place. Sew lace to wrong side of stitched hem, mitering corners.

COUCHING

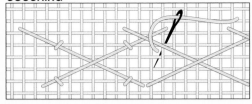

LONG-ARMED CROSS VARIATION

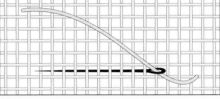

Step 1

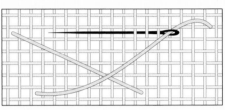

Step 2

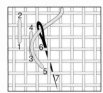

SATIN STITCH

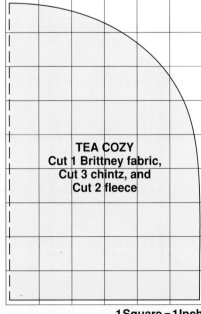

TEA COZY
Cut 1 Brittney fabric,
Cut 3 chintz, and
Cut 2 fleece

1 Square = 1 Inch

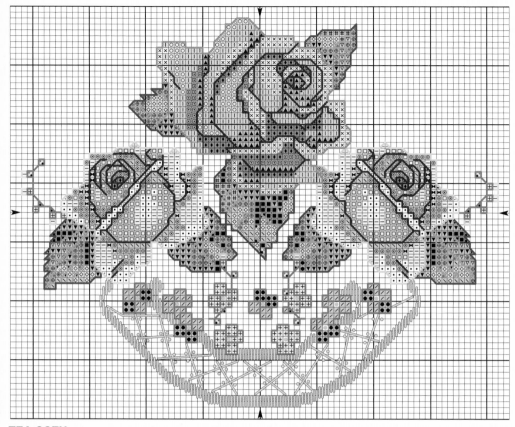

TEA COZY

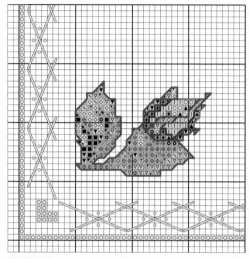

NAPKIN

TEA COZY stitch count: 58 high x 80 wide
TEA COZY finished design sizes:
14-count fabric – 4⅛ x 5¾ inches
11-count fabric – 5¼ x 7¼ inches
9-count fabric – 6½ x 8⅞ inches
NAPKIN stitch count (for rose): 15 high x 24 wide
NAPKIN finished design sizes (for rose):
14-count fabric – 1⅛ x 1¾ inches
11-count fabric – 1⅜ x 2⅛ inches
9-count fabric – 1⅝ x 2⅝ inches

LOVE ONE ANOTHER

ANCHOR		DMC
059	▲	326 Deep rose
1046	◣	435 Light golden brown
1039	☑	518 Wedgwood blue
860	⋈	522 Olive drab
208	⊞	563 Seafoam
167	+	598 Turquoise
890	⊙	729 Old gold
301	□	744 Yellow
275	•	746 Off-white
024	○	776 Medium pink
168	╱	807 Medium peacock blue
1005	▣	816 Light garnet
271	✕	819 Light pink
218	▼	890 Pistachio
052	⊏	899 Light rose
897	◆	902 Deep garnet
851	⊡	924 Gray blue
189	■	991 Dark aquamarine
187	▽	992 Medium aquamarine
292	–	3078 Lemon
268	⊕	3345 Hunter green
266	◇	3347 Yellow green
170	●	3765 Deep peacock blue
868	✳	3779 Terra-cotta

ANCHOR		DMC
BACKSTITCH		
059	╱	326 Deep rose – small hearts (1X)
358	╱	433 Deep golden brown – inner part of yellow roses
1046	╱	435 Light golden brown – letters
208	╱	563 Seafoam – letters
301	╱	744 Yellow – letters, yellow roses
168	╱	807 Medium peacock blue – letters, small blue flowers
052	╱	899 Light rose – inside buds, letters, hearts (1X)
897	╱	902 Deep garnet – inner part of pink roses, buds
189	╱	991 Dark aquamarine – letters
268	╱	3345 Hunter green – leaves
266	╱	3347 Yellow green – leaf centers
170	╱	3765 Deep peacock blue – letters, stems, small blue flowers on tea cozy
868	╱	3779 Terra-cotta – letters

ANCHOR		DMC
FRENCH KNOTS		
023	○	818 Pale pink #12 pearl cotton – border (1X)
292	○	3078 Lemon – center of blue flowers on tea cozy (2X)
SATIN STITCH		
023	❘	818 Pale pink #3 pearl cotton – border (1X)
COUCHING		
023	╱	818 Pale pink #12 pearl cotton – border (1X)

SAMPLER stitch count: 163 high x 258 wide
SAMPLER finished design sizes:
14-count fabric – 11⅝ x 18½ inches
11-count fabric – 14¾ x 23½ inches
9-count fabric – 18 x 28⅝ inches

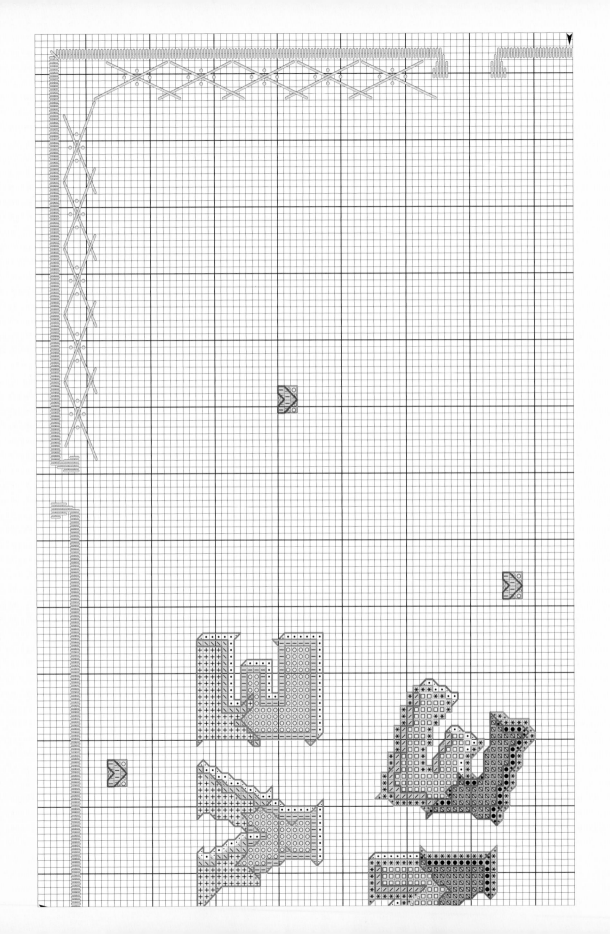

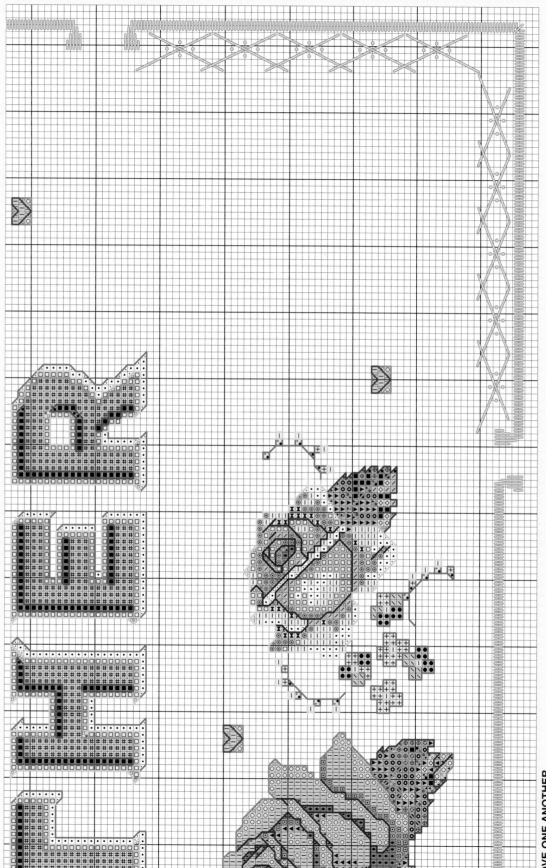

LOVE ONE ANOTHER

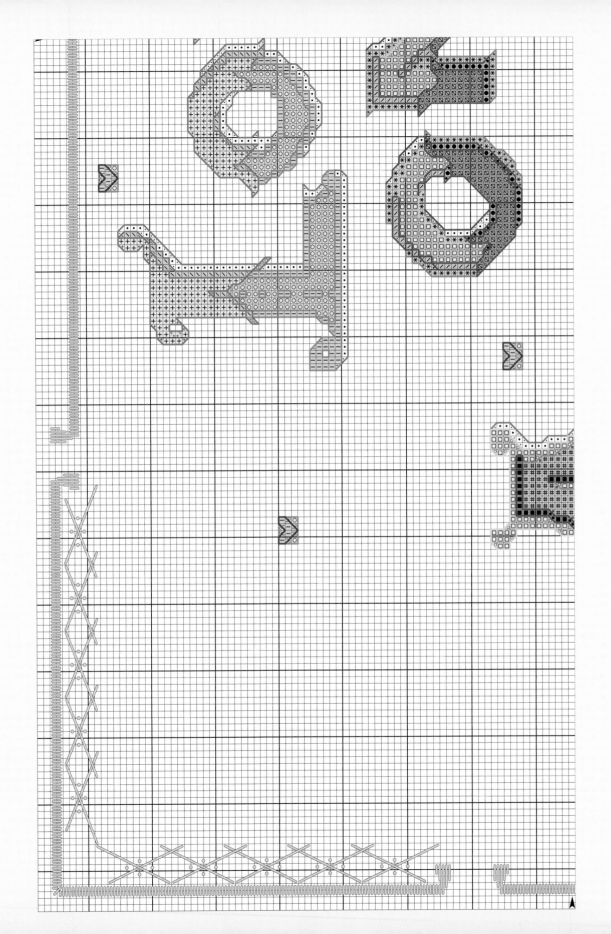

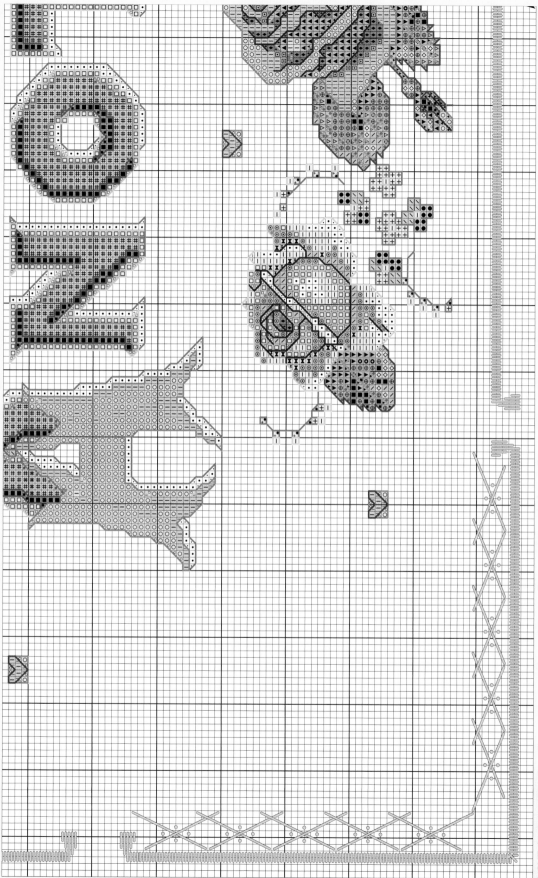

PETITES FLEURS HANDKERCHIEF PILLOW

Vintage Hanky Pillows

In days gone by, a proper lady always had a lovely handkerchief tucked into her purse. These pillow designs capture that charming era. The keys and charts are on pages 102–103.

MATERIALS

FABRIC
15×15-inch piece of 28-count white Jubilee fabric
1 yard of 45-inch-wide taffeta for pillow back
⅛ yard of 45-inch-wide taffeta for ruffle piping

FLOSS
Cotton embroidery floss in colors listed in key
2 additional skeins of medium cornflower blue (DMC 793) for Petites Fleurs pillow
2 additional skeins of parrot green (DMC 906) for either pillow

SUPPLIES
Basting thread; embroidery hoop; needle
Polyester fiberfill
5½ yards of purchased ⅛-inch-diameter cording

INSTRUCTIONS

Tape or zigzag fabric edges. Use basting thread to divide fabric into quarters. Find lower right-hand corner of chart and center of fabric; begin stitching there. Stitch entire chart to complete upper left quarter of design. Work cross-stitches over two threads using two plies of floss. When first quarter is complete, rotate fabric a quarter turn (90 degrees); stitch second quarter in same manner. Stitch remaining half of design, rotating fabric 90 degrees after each quarter. Trim fabric to 13×13 inches.

From taffeta, cut a 13×13-inch pillow back, six 3¾×45-inch ruffle strips, and two 1¼×25-inch piping strips. From ruffle taffeta, cut three 1¼×45-inch piping strips. All measurements include ½-inch seam allowances.

Sew short ends of piping strips together to form a continuous circle. Cut 48 inches of cording; center lengthwise on wrong side of piping strip with cut ends touching. Fold the fabric around cording, bringing raw edges together. Use a zipper foot to sew through both layers of fabric close to cording. Pin covered cording to pillow front, aligning raw edges. Construct piping in same manner, using three piping strips and a 132-inch length of cording.

Sew short ends of three ruffle strips together to form a continuous circle. Repeat with remaining ruffle strips. Pin piping to one edge of one ruffle strip, aligning raw edges. With right sides together, pin remaining ruffle strip on top; sew near stitching line on piping. Turn ruffle; press.

Sew a gathering thread through both layers of ruffle ½ inch from raw edges. Pull threads to fit perimeter of pillow front, with raw edges even; adjust gathers. Sew ruffle to pillow along piping stitching line. Sew pillow front to back with right sides facing, leaving an opening. Clip corners, turn, and press. Stuff firmly; sew opening closed.

AMERICAN BEAUTY
HANDKERCHIEF PILLOW

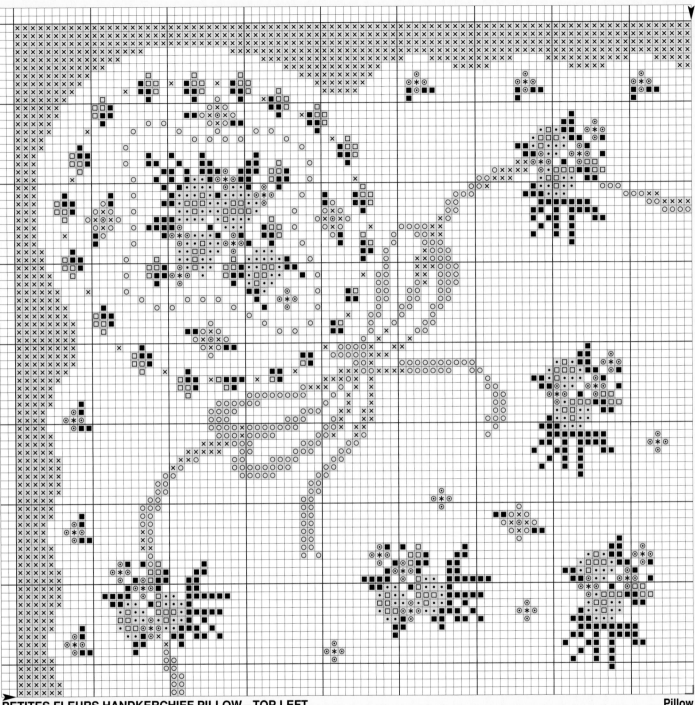

PETITES FLEURS HANDKERCHIEF PILLOW – TOP LEFT

Pillow center

Stitch count: 168 high x 176 wide
Finished design sizes:
14-count fabric – 12¼ x 12¼ inches
11-count fabric – 15⅝ x 15⅝ inches
18-count fabric – 9½ x 9½ inches

PETITES FLEURS HANDKERCHIEF PILLOW

ANCHOR	DMC	
118	●	340 Medium periwinkle
117	□	341 Light periwinkle
176	⊠	793 Medium cornflower blue
175	○	794 Light cornflower blue
256	■	906 Parrot green
054	⊙	956 Geranium
297	✳	973 Canary

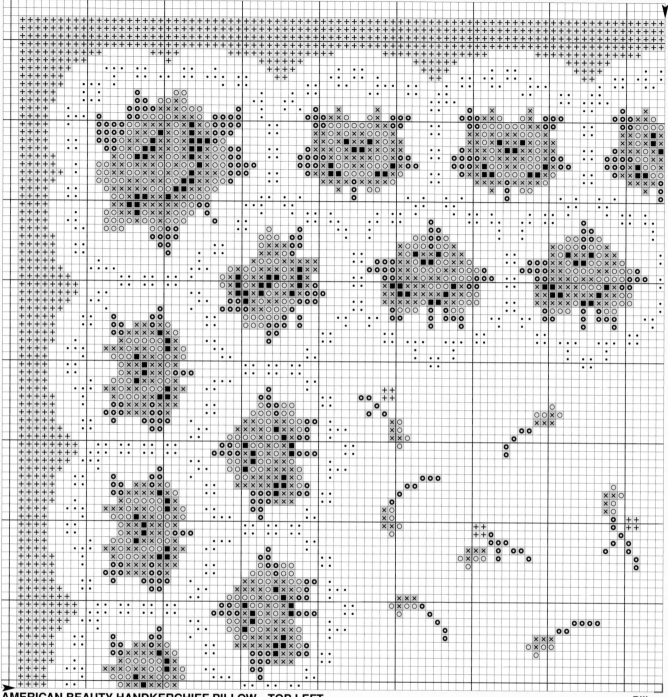

AMERICAN BEAUTY HANDKERCHIEF PILLOW – TOP LEFT

Stitch count: 168 high x 168 wide
Finished design sizes:
14-count fabric – 12 x 12 inches
11-count fabric – 15¼ x 15¼ inches
18-count fabric – 9⅜ x 9⅜ inches

AMERICAN BEAUTY HANDKERCHIEF PILLOW

ANCHOR		DMC
002	·	000 White (2X)
9046	✕	321 Christmas red
1039	+	518 Wedgwood blue
062	⊙	603 Cranberry
043	■	815 Garnet
256	◉	906 Parrot green

Stitched on white linen, this charming piece uses pastel colors and tiny pearl beads. The pansies and bleeding hearts offer a sense of yesteryear.

Floral-Laden Heart

ANCHOR		DMC		ANCHOR		DMC		ANCHOR		DMC	
342	◣	211 Lavender		886	▯	677 Pale old gold		977	╱	334 Dark baby blue – ribbon	
352	■	300 Mahogany		890	✳	729 Medium old gold		860	╱	522 Dark olive drab – small leaves	
215	●	320 True pistachio		275	•	746 Off white					
977	▲	334 Dark baby blue		128	◇	775 Light baby blue		098	╱	553 Medium violet – pansies	
214	▢	368 Light pistachio		075	♥	962 Medium rose pink					
1043	╱	369 Pale pistachio		073	▬	963 Pale rose pink		890	╱	729 Medium old gold – pansies, bleeding hearts	
860	◆	522 Dark olive drab		144	➕	3325 True baby blue					
859	✕	523 Medium olive drab		025	○	3716 Light rose pink		075	╱	962 Medium rose pink – bleeding hearts	
858	▭	524 Light olive drab		140	◉	3755 Medium baby blue					
098	◆	553 Medium violet						**PEARLS**			
096	◉	554 Light violet		**BACKSTITCH**					•	White	
891	▽	676 Light old gold		215	╱	320 True pistachio – large leaves, vines					

MATERIALS

FABRIC AND FLOSS
10×10-inch piece of 28-count white linen; cotton embroidery floss in colors listed in key

SUPPLIES
Needle; embroidery hoop
28 one-mm pearls
Desired mat and frame

INSTRUCTIONS

Tape or zigzag fabric edges. Find center of chart and of fabric; begin stitching there.

Use three plies of floss to work cross-stitches over two threads of fabric. Work backstitches using one ply. Use sewing thread to sew on pearls as shown on chart. Press and frame as desired.

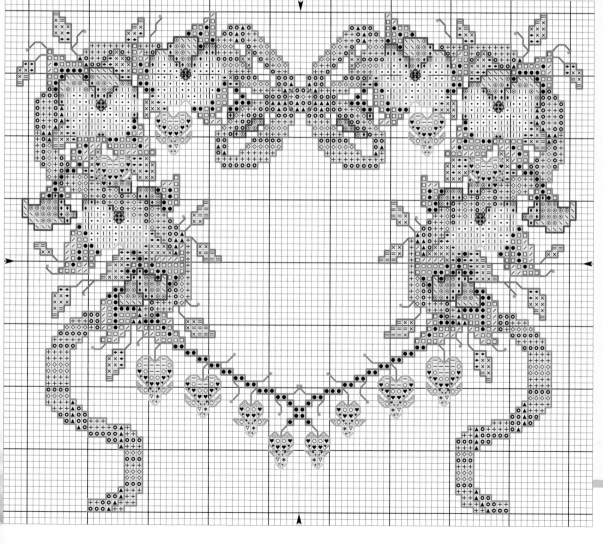

Stitch count: 80 high x 94 wide
Finished design sizes:
14-count fabric – 5³/4 x 6³/4 inches
11-count fabric – 7¹/4 x 8¹/2 inches
18-count fabric – 4¹/2 x 5¹/4 inches

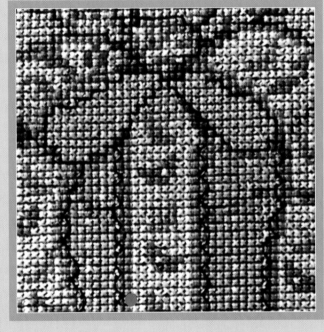

Gracious Gifts

Share your stitching talents with those near and dear. In this chapter you'll discover fun-to-make projects that are perfect for gift giving. Some are so quick, you'll have them finished in an evening, while others require just a little more time. Whichever projects you choose, you'll tell someone just how special they are by presenting them with a gift you created with needle and floss.

Bordering this festive bow-topped package is a sprinkling of small motifs perfect for stitching as gift tags or greeting cards.

The Giving Sampler

MATERIALS

FABRIC
14×14-inch piece of 28-count
black Jobelan

FLOSS
Cotton embroidery floss in colors listed in key

SUPPLIES
Needle; embroidery hoop; desired mat and frame

INSTRUCTIONS

Tape or zigzag fabric edges. Find center of chart and of fabric; begin stitching there. Use three plies of floss to work cross-stitches over two threads of fabric. Work backstitches using one ply. Press the stitchery from the back. Frame as desired.

ANCHOR		DMC	
002	·	000	White
109	⋈	209	Medium lavender
108	✕	210	Light lavender
398	∥	415	Pearl gray
062	⊞	603	True cranberry
074	∧	605	Pale cranberry
324	▽	721	Bittersweet
295	∿	726	Topaz
303	⊓	742	Tangerine
122	▲	792	Cornflower blue
256	⊕	906	Medium parrot green
255	‖	907	Light parrot green
039	◩	961	Rose-pink
292	◿	3078	Lemon
059	★	3350	Dusty rose
120	–	3747	Periwinkle
176	✳	3839	Medium lavender-blue
120	○	3840	Light lavender-blue

BACKSTITCH (1X)

108	╱	210 Light lavender – lavender ribbon, "To," "From," package
295	╱	726 Topaz – tag
303	╱	742 Tangerine – package
122	╱	792 Cornflower blue – top blue ribbon, package top
258	╱	904 Deep parrot green – stems, rose leaves
059	╱	3350 Dusty rose – rose, hearts, "With Love"
176	╱	3839 Medium lavender-blue – blue ribbon, butterfly outline and antennae, large "For You," package
403	╱	310 Black – all remaining stitches

FRENCH KNOT

108	◯	210 Light lavender – colons
176	◯	3839 Medium lavender-blue – exclamation dot

Stitch count: 101 high x 101 wide
Finished design sizes:
28-count fabric – 7 1/8 x 7 1/8 inches
32-count fabric – 6 3/8 x 6 3/8 inches
36-count fabric – 5 2/3 x 5 2/3 inches

Pretty Pansy Greetings

A gift in itself, this sweet note card will express thoughtful wishes to anyone who receives it. A window cut from a blank note card makes finishing easy.

MATERIALS

FABRIC
7×6-inch piece of 14-count black perforated paper

FLOSS
Cotton embroidery floss in colors listed in key

SUPPLIES
Needle; crafts knife; thick white crafts glue
4½×5½-inch piece of black construction paper
7×5-inch ivory note card and envelope
6¾×4¾-inch piece of ivory construction paper

INSTRUCTIONS

Find the center of the chart and the center of the perforated paper; begin stitching there. Use three plies of floss to work the cross-stitches. Work straight stitches and backstitches using one ply of floss.

Center black construction paper on back side of stitched piece and glue at outer edges only. Trim stitched piece even with construction paper.

Open note card. On card front, measure and cut a 5×4-inch opening in center using a crafts knife. Center stitched piece in opening and glue to card at outer edges. Glue ivory construction paper to back side of the stitchery.

ANCHOR		DMC	
002	•	000	White
342	−	211	Lavender
218	●	319	Dark pistachio
978	▲	322	Navy
217	◩	367	Medium pistachio
214			368	Light pistachio
099	■	552	Dark violet
096	♡	554	Light violet
926	○	712	Cream
885	▽	739	Tan
302	▢	743	True yellow
300	+	745	Light yellow
140	✳	3755	Baby blue
928	◺	3811	Turquoise
306	△	3820	Dark straw
874	╱	3822	Light straw

BACKSTITCH

002	╱	000	White – lettering
380	╱	838	Beige brown – all remaining stitches

STRAIGHT STITCH

380	╱	838	Beige brown – pansy interiors

Stitch count: 71 high x 55 wide
Finished design sizes:
14-count fabric – 5 x 4 inches
18-count fabric – 4 x 3 inches
8½-count fabric – 8⅓ x 6⅜ inches

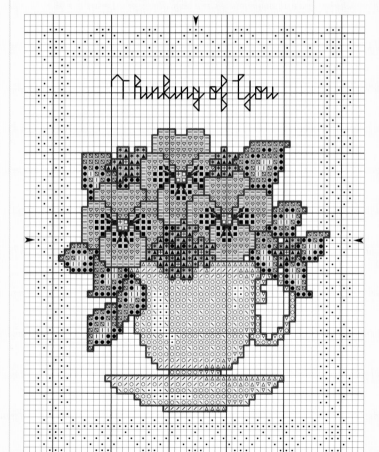

Old-Fashioned Seed Packet

A glorious profusion of colorful zinnias brightens the front of this clever bag that was inspired by a modest seed packet. The finished stitchery is fused to cotton fabric, then sewn into a bag shape. Fill the finished bag with dried flowers or place a vase of fresh blossoms into the bag for a delightful floral arrangement. The chart and key are on pages 114–115.

MATERIALS

FABRIC
16×23-inch piece of 28-count star sapphire linen
16×23-inch piece floral print cotton fabric
16×23-inch piece paper-backed iron-on adhesive

FLOSS
Cotton embroidery floss in colors listed in key on page 115
Overdyed floss in colors listed in key on page 115

SUPPLIES
Needle; embroidery hoop
Seed beads in colors listed in key on page 115
Erasable marker
Pinking shears
Matching sewing thread

INSTRUCTIONS

Tape or zigzag edges of fabric to prevent fraying. With 23-inch edge of fabric at top, find the center of the chart and the center of the fabric; begin stitching there.

Use two plies of floss to work cross-stitches over two threads of fabric. Work satin stitches using four plies of overdyed floss. Work French knots using two plies of floss. Work backstitches using one ply of floss. Use one ply of navy floss to sew beads to flower centers.

Fuse iron-on adhesive to the wrong side of linen. Remove the paper backing and fuse to the cotton fabric following the manufacturer's instructions. All measurements include a ½-inch seam allowance.

Measure 2½ inches beyond top edge of purple triangle at top of design; use marker to draw a line parallel to top of triangle the width of the fabric. Trim excess fabric with pinking shears.

With the design centered left to right, use scissors to trim remaining sides to make an 11×16-inch bag. From excess fabric, cut one 3½×6½ bag bottom. Sew the 11-inch edges of bag together, with the right sides facing, to form a tube. Turn right side out. Lay tube flat on ironing board. Press a crease from top to bottom edge just beyond the right edge of the purple triangle. Press another crease in the fabric where fabric folds at opposite edge of the tube.

Refold the tube and press another crease ¼ inch to the left of the stitched design and on the fold at the opposite edge. Be careful not to press out the first pair of creases. Turn the bag wrong side out.

Beginning at one corner, sew one long edge of the bag bottom to the lower edge of the bag with right sides together, clipping and pivoting bottom piece at the corners. Turn the bag right side out. Fold over the top edge 1 inch to the outside of the bag.

OLD-FASHIONED SEED PACKET

OLD-FASHIONED SEED PACKET

ANCHOR		DMC	
118	☒	340	Periwinkle
059	◆	600	Deep cranberry
063	⊕	602	Medium cranberry
062	★	603	True cranberry
332	▲	608	Orange
305	◙	725	Topaz
316	⊞	740	Dark tangerine
314	Ⅰ	741	Medium tangerine
303	▫	742	Light tangerine
300	─	745	Yellow
127	■	823	Navy
1029	◩	915	Dark plum
089	⊞	917	Medium plum
087	⊙	3607	Fuchsia
035	◆	3705	Dark watermelon
033	◪	3706	Medium watermelon
031	◎	3708	Light watermelon
	⊡	164	Needle Necessities Santa Fe overdyed floss
	⁄	182	Needle Necessities sandstone overdyed floss

BACKSTITCH

127	╱	823	Navy– lettering, border
382	╱	3371	Black brown– flowers

DIAGONAL SATIN STITCH
(stitch in direction of symbol)

	╱	139	Needle Necessities mountain spruce overdyed floss

FRENCH KNOT

127	●	823	Navy–flower centers

BEADS

	✕	03026	Wild blueberry Mill Hill antique seed bead– flower centers

Stitch count: 116 high x 71 wide

Finished design sizes:
14-count fabric – 8¼ x 5 inches
11-count fabric – 10½ x 6½ inches
8½-count fabric –13⅝ x 8⅜ inches

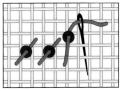

Attaching a Bead

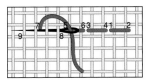

Backstitch

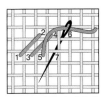

Diagonal Satin Stitch

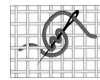

French Knot

Victorian Bookmark

Treat yourself to the luxury of exquisite silk ribbons. Drawn-thread ribbon weaving is an easy-to-learn method for combining these beautiful ribbons with cross-stitch. This Victorian-style bookmark features a frame of adobe silk around a garland of salmon-colored roses. Finish the bookmark with a sparkly beaded fringe. The chart and key are on page 119.

MATERIALS

FABRIC
14×8-inch piece of 28-count wood violet linen
7¼×4¼-inch piece of 28-count wood violet linen

FLOSS
Cotton embroidery in colors listed in key
on page 119

SUPPLIES
Tapestry, sewing, and beading needles
Embroidery hoop
1½ yards 4-millimeter adobe (YLI 088) silk ribbon
Sewing thread to match fabric
Mill Hill seed beads: peach crème (02003),
purple (62042), amethyst (03034), and
royal green (03035)
Mill Hill large bugle beads: sapphire (90168)
Mill Hill medium bugle beads: sapphire (80168)
and purple (82051)
Mill Hill small bugle beads: peach (72003) and
purple (72051)

INSTRUCTIONS

Tape or zigzag edges of larger piece of fabric. Find vertical center of chart. Measure 1½ inches from narrow end (top) of fabric. Begin stitching center row of top single rose there. Use two plies of floss to work cross-stitches and backstitches over two threads of linen.

Run a basting thread as indicated by the dotted line marked on the chart to designate finished edge of bookmark. Trim fabric ½ inch beyond basting stitches across top edge and along both long sides. Trim bottom edge 6 inches from basting stitches.

To remove threads, count six threads below the top single rose. With a tapestry needle, lift and remove the next four horizontal threads from the linen. (Five horizontal threads will remain between the pulled threads and the top of center garland of roses.) Count four threads above single rose at the bottom. Remove the next four horizontal threads. To pull vertical threads, count 10 threads to the right of the last cross-stitch on the right; remove next four vertical threads. Repeat for left side.

For ribbon weaving, cut two 8-inch and two 12-inch ribbon lengths. Use one short ribbon to work running stitches over four threads and under one through upper horizontal band. Repeat for lower horizontal band. Use long ribbons to complete vertical bands. Trim ribbon ends even with linen.

Remove horizontal threads for 6 inches at lower edge of bookmark to create fringe. Finger-press top and side seams under along basting stitches. Carefully cut away the fringe from the side seam allowances.

On smaller fabric rectangle, finger-press ½-inch seam allowances on all edges. Overcast edges together using matching thread. With wrong sides facing, stitch the two rectangles together. If desired, use tiny topstitches across the bottom edge.

continued on page 118

For beaded fringe, thread beads on the 6-inch linen threads. Work two strands of beaded fringe outside each strand of ribbon and 17 strands, evenly spaced, between the ribbons. Thread remaining linen threads between the bookmark layers.

Thread beading needle with one linen thread. Add beads in the following sequence: sapphire medium bugle, purple seed, amethyst seed, purple seed, sapphire large bugle, purple seed, amethyst seed, purple seed, purple medium bugle, peach seed, royal green seed, peach seed, peach small bugle, peach seed, royal green seed, peach seed, amethyst seed, purple small bugle, amethyst seed. Finish with seven royal green seed beads. Slip thread through bottom of the first of the seven royal green seed beads, forming a small loop. Knot thread around bead, then slip thread up through about 1 inch of the strung beads; clip thread.

Alternate this pattern of beading with the following: sapphire medium bugle, purple seed, royal green seed, purple seed, sapphire large bugle, purple seed, royal green seed, purple seed, purple medium bugle, peach seed, amethyst seed, peach seed, peach small bugle, amethyst seed, peach seed, amethyst seed, purple small bugle, royal green seed. Finish in the same manner as the first pattern with seven amethyst seed beads.

To finish, cut a 16-inch length of ribbon. Pinch a ¾-inch loop 2 inches from one end. Press the loop flat toward end. Tack in place, then tack to one intersection of woven ribbons at the top of the bookmark. Repeat for opposite side.

LEFT: *After locating the threads to be removed, slide a tapestry needle to a point about 1 inch from the edge of the fabric. Slip the needle under one thread and pull upward, putting tension on the thread until one end pulls out of the fabric.*

CENTER: *Pull on the loose thread with one hand while pushing the fabric into loose gathers with the other hand. Work the gathers toward the opposite end until the thread can be completely removed.*

RIGHT: *Thread the needle with silk ribbon. Slide needle under one of the cross threads remaining after pulling. Skip four threads; slide needle under next single thread. Repeat this pattern across to opposite edge.*

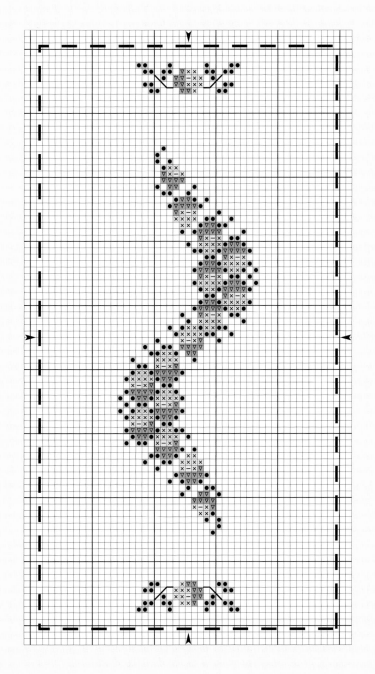

VICTORIAN BOOKMARK

ANCHOR		DMC	
1014	▽	355	Terra-cotta
302	−	743	Yellow
189	●	991	Aquamarine
1023	✕	3712	Salmon

BACKSTITCH

189	/	991	Aquamarine – top, bottom stems

Stitch count: 86 high x 23 wide

Finished design sizes:
14-count fabric – 6¹/₈ x 1⁵/₈ inches
10-count fabric – 8⁵/₈ x 2³/₈ inches
18-count fabric – 4³/₄ x 1¹/₄ inches

Floral Chatelaine

A lovely necessity for anyone who enjoys needlework, this cross-stitched chatelaine is pretty as well as functional. Hanging from the glistening gold chain are special attachments to keep all supplies at hand. Stitch this perfect project on 32-count natural linen. To make finishing easy and more professional, you'll find helpful hints on page 122. The charts and key are on page 123.

MATERIALS

FABRICS FOR SCISSORS CASE
13×13-inch piece of 32-count natural linen
13×13-inch piece of desired cotton fabric
FABRICS FOR NEEDLE CASE
10×10-inch piece of 32-count natural linen for book cover
3½×4½-inch piece of 32-count natural linen for pages
FABRIC FOR TAPE MEASURE CASE
14×14-inch piece of 32-count natural linen
FABRIC FOR THIMBLE CASE
5×5-inch piece of 32-count natural linen
FABRIC FOR PINCUSHION
6×2½-inch piece of cotton fabric

FLOSS
Cotton embroidery floss in colors listed in key on page 123

SUPPLIES
Needle; embroidery hoop
Cotton ball or small piece of batting
3 yards of ⅛-inch-wide pink satin ribbon
Scrap of fiberfill
32-inch piece of gold jewelry chain
Matching thread; silver finding
Needle emery powder
(purchase from marble or rock polishing shop)

INSTRUCTIONS

Tape or zigzag edges of fabric to prevent fraying. Working over two threads, use two plies of floss for cross-stitches and one ply for the backstitches. Measurements include a ¼-inch seam allowance.

For scissors case, finger-press fabric in half with edges together; open. With fold line at left edge, find center of right half of fabric and center of chart; begin stitching entire piece there. With right sides together, refold scissors case on fold line. Stitch side seam ¼ inch from stitching; trim. Trim open edge of case ½ inch from stitching. Fold lining fabric in half with edges together. Use stitched piece as a pattern to cut lining.

Sew side seam of lining, leaving a 2-inch section unstitched in center of side seam for turning. Tuck stitched piece into lining and stitch together at top. Pull stitched piece through opening. Insert cotton ball through opening; push it firmly into point of stitched scissors case. Slip-stitch opening closed and tuck lining into case. Cut a 10-inch length of ribbon; knot ends together. Tack to inside of case at top right corner.

For needle case, finger press fabric in half with edges together; open. With fold line at top, find the center of bottom half of fabric and the center of chart; begin stitching entire piece there. Measure 1 inch below bottom row of stitching; trim there. From cut line, measure 5¾ inches up; trim. Finger-press ½ inch under on each edge of stitched piece; miter the corners and tack in place. Turn under ¼ inch on lining; miter corners. With wrong sides facing, center lining on stitched piece; stitch in place.

continued on page 122

Zigzag edges of linen for needle book pages. For invisible stitching, pull a 10-inch thread from fabric scrap; thread through needle. Center pages over lining; stitch down center through all layers. Cut a 10-inch length from ribbon; knot ends. Tack to inside of case at center top.

For tape measure case, finger-press the fabric in half with edges together; open. With fold line at the left, find the center of the right side of fabric and the center of design; begin stitching entire piece there. With right sides together, trim fabric ½ inch from the edge of stitching. Stitch bottom and remaining side ¼ inch from stitching; trim. Turn top under ¼ inch. Turn under again; stitch in place. Cut an 8-inch length from ribbon; knot ends. Tack to the inside of the case at each corner at top.

For thimble case, finger-press fabric in half; open. With fold line at bottom, find the center of top half of fabric and the center of design; begin stitching there. With right sides together, fold fabric ¼ inch from edge of stitching. Stitch sides ¼ inch from stitching; trim. Turn top under ¼ inch. Turn under again and stitch in place.

Cut 5-inch length from ribbon; knot ends. Tack to inside of case at each top corner.

For pincushion, fold rectangle in half with long edges together. Sew bottom and side seam; turn. Fold under ¼ inch on open end. Fill with fiberfill. Refold top of pincushion with seam even with fold line; stitch opening closed. Cut 5-inch length from ribbon; tie ends into bow. Tack to top left corner.

For needle sharpener, cut fabric using pattern, *opposite*. Sew side seam using ¼-inch seams. Clip seam; turn. Stitch basting line ½ inch from top. Fill triangular pocket with needle emery powder to basting line. Pull basting thread to close; clip extra fabric. Sew opening closed. Stitch silver finding to top of needle sharpener. Thread 7-inch piece of ribbon through hole at top of sharpener. Tie ends into bow; tack to lower right corner of pincushion.

Cut chain to desired length. Slip ribbon loops of attachments through ends of chain. Bring attachments back through loops to secure.

TIPS FOR FINISHING

LEFT: INVISIBLE STITCHING
For invisible hand stitching, as used to sew the pages to the needle book, pull a thread from leftover fabric.
MIDDLE LEFT: STITCHING A LINING
For a professional lining, stitch the side seam of the lining piece leaving an opening in the center of the seam. Turn through opening. Stitch the opening closed.

MIDDLE RIGHT AND RIGHT: MITERING CORNERS
Step One: *After trimming fabric, fold in corner. Align the fabric edge on the turned corner with the fabric weave.*
Step Two: *Fold sides in at corner to meet in the center. Tack in place.*

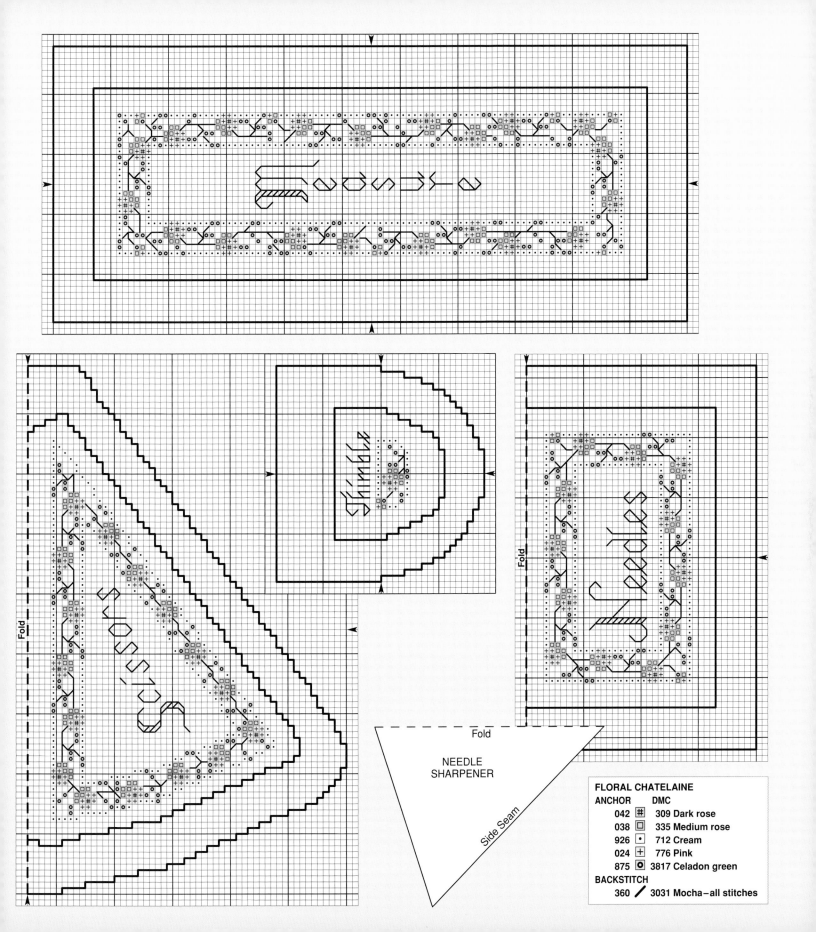

Fold

NEEDLE
SHARPENER

Side Seam

FLORAL CHATELAINE

ANCHOR		DMC	
042	⊞	309	Dark rose
038	☐	335	Medium rose
926	•	712	Cream
024	+	776	Pink
875	⊙	3817	Celadon green

BACKSTITCH

| 360 | ╱ | 3031 | Mocha–all stitches |

Handmade Labels

Add an extra special personal touch to all your handmade projects with tiny cross-stitched labels. The motifs are stitched on 32-count Belfast linen and work up easily. Use the various motifs and alphabets to create a stack of labels as a gift for a crafting friend.

MATERIALS

FABRIC FOR ALL LABELS
12×6-inch piece of 32-count white Belfast linen
12×6-inch piece of fusible interfacing

FLOSS
Cotton embroidery floss in desired colors, using key as a guide

SUPPLIES
Graph paper
Needle; embroidery hoop
#8 pearl cotton to coordinate with design

INSTRUCTIONS

Tape or zigzag edges of fabric to prevent fraying. Combine and chart desired motifs, referring to chart, *below*. Find center of charted design and center of fabric; begin stitching there.

Use two plies of floss for all cross-stitches. Work backstitches, straight stitches, lazy daisy stitches, and French knots as specified in key.

Cut fabric ¼ inch beyond each side of design. Use this as a pattern to cut interfacing. Fuse interfacing to back of design following the manufacturer's directions.

To finish, use the buttonhole stitch to complete the edges of the design, using #8 pearl cotton in a coordinating color.

⊡ Color 1		**STRAIGHT STITCH**
☒ Color 2		╱ Color A
▲ Color 3		╱ Color B
▽ Color 4		**LAZY DAISY**
BACKSTITCH		⊘ Color A – lamb (2X)
╱ Color A		⊘ Color B – heart with needle (2X)
╱ Color B		**FRENCH KNOT**
		● Color A (2X)

Sew a Fine Seam

Use 18-count oatmeal Rustico fabric and a purchased 5½x5½-inch black wooden box to make this elegant sewing container. Create the chatelaine as an accessory to keep your thimble and scissors nearby. The chart and key are on page 129.

MATERIALS
FOR THE WOOD BOX

FABRIC
9×9-inch piece of 18-count oatmeal Rustico fabric

FLOSS
Cotton embroidery floss in colors listed in key on page 129

SUPPLIES
Needle; embroidery hoop
5½×5½-inch black wood box with framed lid for stitchery insertion

INSTRUCTIONS
FOR THE WOOD BOX

Tape or zigzag the edges of fabric to prevent fraying. Find the center of the chart and the center of the fabric; begin stitching there.

Working over two threads, use two plies of floss to work cross-stitches and French knots. Work backstitches using one ply unless otherwise specified in key. Assemble box following manufacturer's instructions.

MATERIALS
FOR THE CHATELAINE

FABRICS FOR THE THIMBLE HOLDER
Two 5×5-inch pieces of 18-count oatmeal Rustico fabric; two 4×4-inch pieces of red cotton fabric

FABRICS FOR THE SCISSORS CASE
Two 5×3-inch pieces of 18-count oatmeal Rustico fabric
Two 5×3-inch pieces of red cotton fabric

FLOSS
Cotton embroidery floss in colors listed in key on page 129

SUPPLIES
Needle; embroidery hoop
2 yards of 1-inch-wide red grosgrain ribbon

Erasable marker
Two ¾-inch-wide vest buckles
Red sewing thread
Four ¼-inch-diameter red buttons
Three ⅜-inch-diameter white buttons
Small red strawberry needle emery
2½ yards of ⅛-inch-wide red satin ribbon
Scissors; other desired accessories

INSTRUCTIONS
FOR THE THIMBLE HOLDER

Zigzag the edges of fabric to prevent fraying. Find the lower left-hand corner of chart. On bottom of Rustico fabric, measure 1½ inches in from left edge and 1½ inches from bottom; begin stitching leaf/flower/strawberry motif there.

Use two plies of floss to work cross-stitches over two threads. Work backstitches using one ply of floss. Using white floss, cross-stitch two rows at bottom and left edge, positioning one row up and one row in from outermost stitches. Stitch these rows until stitched area reaches a count of 36 high × 36 wide. Fill in square using grid motif from chart. Trim ½ inch from

continued on page 128

stitching. Use stitched piece as a pattern to cut one back from remaining Rustico fabric and two lining pieces from red fabric.

Sew thimble holder front to back, using ¼-inch seams; leave top edge open. Sew lining pieces together in the same manner, except leave an opening at bottom; do not turn.

Cut a 7-inch piece of ribbon; slip-stitch ends of ribbon to top of holder at sides. Stitch holder to lining at top edge. Turn right side out. Slip-stitch opening closed; press. Set aside.

INSTRUCTIONS
FOR THE SCISSORS CASE

Zigzag the edges of the fabric. Find grid motif on chart and center of one piece of Rustico fabric; stitch a 1×3-inch area of grid pattern.

Work stitches as directed for thimble holder. With one short stitched end at left, use erasable marker to draw from left corners to center of right end. Cut out ½ inch from lines. Attach buttons as desired. Use stitched piece as a pattern to cut one back from the remaining Rustico fabric and two lining pieces from the red fabric.

Sew case front to back, leaving top edge open. Sew lining pieces together in same manner, except leave an opening at bottom; do not turn. Stitch case to lining at top edge. Turn right side out. Slip-stitch opening closed and press.

INSTRUCTIONS
TO ASSEMBLE THE CHATELAINE

Fold grosgrain ribbon in half and sew together along long edges. Slip vest buckles onto ribbon, ending 7 inches from ribbon ends.

Fold a 7-inch piece of satin ribbon in half and sew to the top of strawberry emery. Cut four 12-inch pieces of satin ribbon. With ends even, tie two ribbons into a bow. Repeat with remaining ribbons; trim ends. Tack bows to top of strawberry emery.

Press ends of grosgrain ribbon under ¼ inch; fold under ½ inch. Place hanging ribbons of thimble holder and strawberry emery at fold; hand-stitch grosgrain ribbon together. Repeat for opposite end, placing remaining satin ribbon at fold; tie ribbon onto scissors.

SEW A FINE SEAM

ANCHOR		DMC
002	·	000 White
1006	⋈	304 Christmas red
011	▢	350 Coral
266	✕	471 Avocado
305	✳	725 True topaz
293	–	727 Pale topaz
244	●	987 Medium forest green
242	△	989 Pale forest green
328	+	3341 Melon
869	╱	3743 Pale antique violet

ANCHOR		DMC
BACKSTITCH		
1006	╱	304 Christmas red – sewing line thread in saying (2X)
871	╱	3041 Medium antique violet – lattice shadow
359	╱	801 Coffee brown – "S," strawberry seeds (2X); all remaining stitches
FRENCH KNOT		
307	•	783 Christmas gold – flower centers (2X)
359	●	801 Coffee brown – saying (2X)

Stitch count: 75 high x 75 wide

Finished design sizes:
14-count fabric – 5⅜ x 5⅜ inches
18-count fabric – 4¼ x 4¼ inches
11-count fabric – 6⅞ x 6⅞ inches

Birthday Jewelry Bags

Say "Happy Birthday" with tiny bags featuring the month's flowers and gemstones. Measuring just 5×4¼ inches, the bags are wonderful wraps for small surprises. The charts and keys begin on page 132.

MATERIALS
FOR EACH BAG

FABRIC
10×16-inch piece of 18-count damask Aida cloth: January, carnation pink; February, dawn gray; March, ivory; April, ice blue; May, ice blue; June, carnation pink; July, dawn gray; August, ivory; September, carnation pink; October, dawn gray; November, ivory; December, ice blue
10×16-inch piece of white cotton fabric

FLOSS
Cotton embroidery floss in colors listed in key on pages 132–137

SUPPLIES
Graph paper; needle; embroidery hoop
7-inch piece of ¾-inch-wide white flat lace
15-inch piece of ¼-inch-wide picot-edged satin ribbon
10×14mm acrylic oval glue-on jewels: January, garnet; February, amethyst; March, aquamarine; April, diamond; May, emerald; June, pearl; July, ruby; August, peridot; September, sapphire; October, opal; November, topaz; December, turquoise
Erasable fabric marker; crafts glue

INSTRUCTIONS

Enlarge pattern, *page 134,* using graph paper; cut out. The pattern includes ¼-inch seam allowances. Pieces are sewn with right sides facing unless otherwise specified. Use erasable marker to trace bag front and back on Aida cloth; do not cut out. Cut lining pieces from white fabric; set aside.

For bag back, turn the Aida cloth with the flap (curved edge) at the bottom. Find center of back chart and of bag back; begin stitching the bottom of the jewel motif ½ inch from bottom of flap outline. Use two plies of floss to work cross-stitches over two threads of fabric. Work French knots and backstitches using one ply.

For bag front, find the vertical center of chart and of bag front; begin stitching bottom edge of flower name 1¼ inches from bottom of bag outline. When stitching is complete, cut out pieces along marked lines.

Sew bag front to back, leaving top and flap edges open. (Lettering on the flap will be upside down.) Sew lining pieces together in the same manner, leaving an opening at bottom; do not trim.

To shape bottom, fold one corner flat so that the bottom and the side seams meet. Stitch perpendicular to the seam lines, ⅜ inch from the fold. Trim the corners. Repeat for opposite corner and for the corners of lining.

Baste the straight edge of the lace ¼ inch from edge of flap. Stitch the bag to the lining at the top edge of the front and around the flap.

Turn; slip-stitch opening closed. Tuck lining into bag.

Tie a bow in center of the ribbon and slip-stitch the ends of the ribbon to the top of the bag at the sides.

Fold the bag and lining together at inside top edge to make a tuck around ribbon. Stitch to secure. Press flap over top of bag front. Glue the acrylic jewel to the bag flap over the stitched jewel.

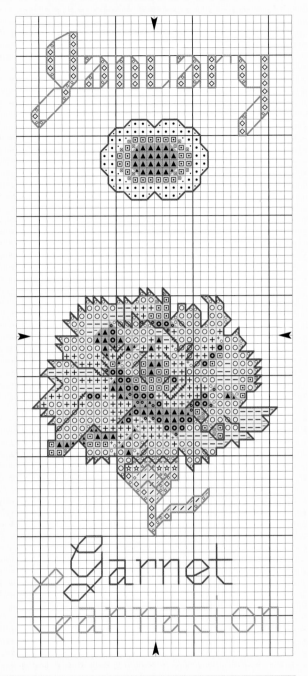

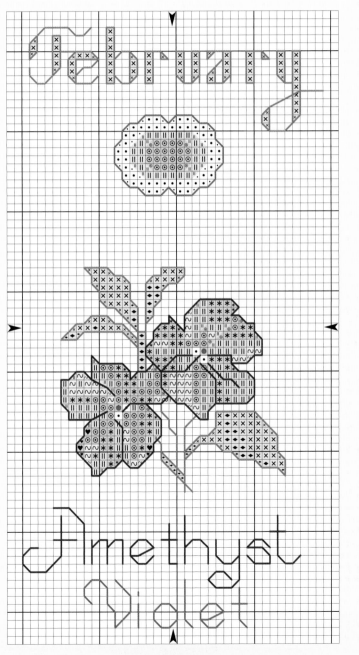

FEBRUARY BIRTHDAY JEWELRY BAG

ANCHOR		DMC		ANCHOR		DMC
387	⊡	Ecru				
109	⊞	209 Lavender		**BACKSTITCH**		
267	◆	469 Dark avocado		267	╱	469 Dark avocado–
102	♥	550 Deep violet				leaves, stems,
099	⊙	552 Dark violet				February lettering
261	☒	3053 Light gray green		102	╱	550 Deep violet–
085	∼	3609 Light fuchsia				flowers, amethyst lettering
BLENDED NEEDLE				099	╱	552 Dark violet–
099	✳	552 Dark violet (1X) and				jewel, violet lettering
089		917 Plum (1X)		**FRENCH KNOT**		
				035	●	3705 Watermelon–
						flower centers

Stitch count: 75 high x 39 wide

Finished design size: 4¹⁄₈ x 2¹⁄₈ inches

JANUARY BIRTHDAY JEWELRY BAG

ANCHOR		DMC		ANCHOR		DMC
387	⊡	Ecru		**BACKSTITCH**		
042	◉	309 Dark rose		877	╱	502 Medium blue green–
024	⊟	776 Medium pink				flower stem,
052	⊞	899 Light rose				January lettering
076	⊡	961 Dark rose pink		076	╱	961 Dark rose pink–
073	◯	963 Pale rose pink				carnation lettering
206	╱	966 Baby green		1028	╱	3685 Mauve–
186	◇	993 Light aquamarine				remaining stitches
264	☆	3348 Yellow green		*Stitch count:* 76 high x 32 wide		
1028	▲	3685 Mauve		*Finished design size:* 4¹⁄₄ x 1³⁄₄ inches		

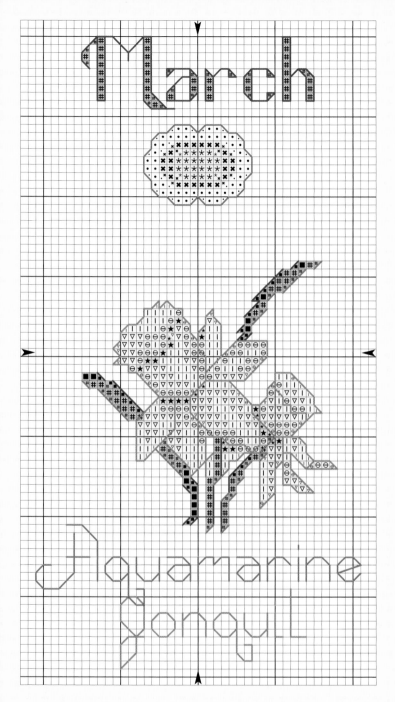

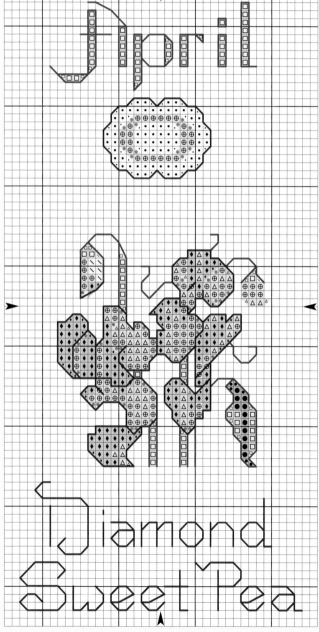

APRIL BIRTHDAY JEWELRY BAG

ANCHOR		DMC	ANCHOR		DMC
387	·	Ecru			BACKSTITCH
118	△	340 Periwinkle	118	/	340 Periwinkle – diamond lettering
1043	◺	369 Pale pistachio	683	/	500 Deep blue green – leaves, April lettering
683	●	500 Deep blue green	178	/	791 Deep cornflower blue – flowers
177	◆	792 Dark cornflower blue	177	/	792 Dark cornflower blue – jewel, sweet pea lettering
136	⊕	799 Delft blue			
187	▱	992 Medium aquamarine			

Stitch count: 76 high x 37 wide

Finished design size: 4¼ x 2 inches

MARCH BIRTHDAY JEWELRY BAG

ANCHOR		DMC	ANCHOR		DMC
387	·	Ecru			BACKSTITCH
1039	✶	518 Wedgwood blue	1039	/	518 Wedgwood blue – jewel, aquamarine lettering
212	⊞	561 Seafoam	212	/	561 Seafoam – lighter side of leaves
167	✕	598 Medium turquoise			
293	⊖	727 Pale topaz	308	/	782 Medium topaz – flowers, jonquil lettering
302	▽	743 True yellow			
308	★	782 Medium topaz	851	/	924 Gray blue – darker side of leaves, March lettering
851	■	924 Gray blue			
292	I	3078 Pale lemon			

Stitch count: 79 high x 37 wide

Finished design size: 4⅜ x 2⅜ inches

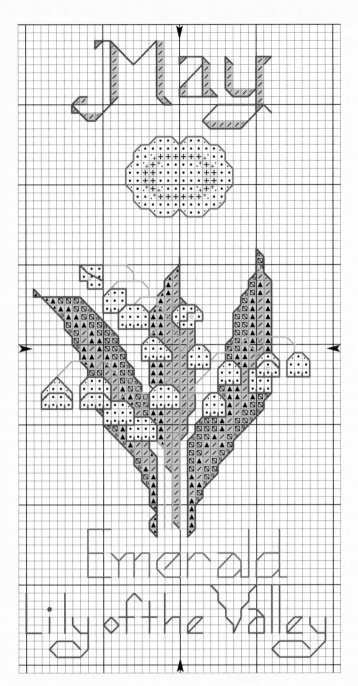

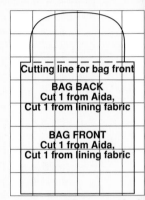

1 Square = 1 Inch

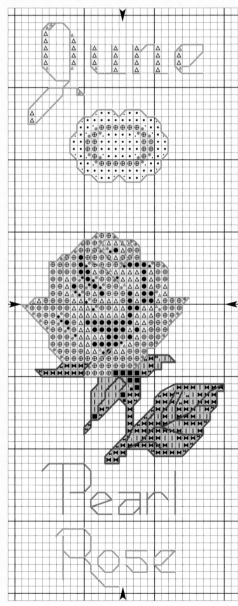

JUNE BIRTHDAY JEWELRY BAG

ANCHOR		DMC		ANCHOR		DMC	
387	·	Ecru		**BACKSTITCH**			
862	■	520 Olive drab		862	╱	520 Olive drab – leaves	
024	⊕	776 Pink		024	╱	776 Pink – jewel	
052	△	899 Rose		243	╱	988 Light forest green – pearl lettering	
244	⋈	987 Medium forest green		076	╱	3731 Dusty rose – June lettering, flower, rose lettering	
243	I	988 Light forest green					
076	●	3731 Dusty rose					

Stitch count: 78 high x 29 wide

Finished design size: 4³⁄₈ x 1⁵⁄₈ inches

MAY BIRTHDAY JEWELRY BAG

ANCHOR		DMC		ANCHOR		DMC	
387	·	Ecru		186	╱	959 Medium aqua – stems	
212	▲	561 Seafoam		170	╱	3765 Peacock blue – flowers, lily of the valley lettering	
188	◩	943 Dark aqua					
186	+	959 Medium aqua		**FRENCH KNOT**			
170	▨	3765 Peacock blue		288	•	445 Lemon – centers of flowers	
BACKSTITCH				170	●	3765 Peacock blue – lily of the valley lettering	
212	╱	561 Seafoam – May lettering, leaves					
188	╱	943 Dark aqua – jewel, emerald lettering					

Stitch count: 77 high x 39 wide

Finished design size: 4³⁄₈ x 2¹⁄₈ inches

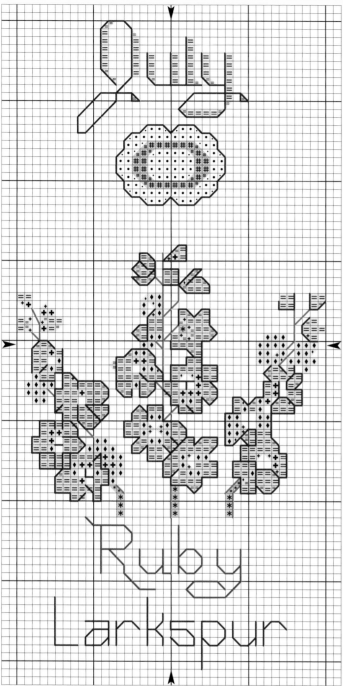

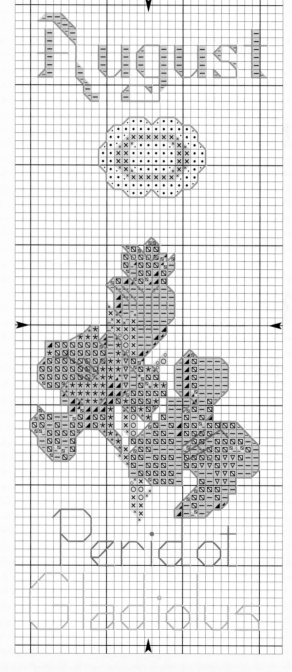

AUGUST BIRTHDAY JEWELRY BAG

ANCHOR		DMC	ANCHOR		DMC
387	•	Ecru	BACKSTITCH		
010	–	351 Coral	010	/	351 Coral – gladiolus lettering
214	✕	368 Pistachio	214	/	368 Pistachio – jewel
266	○	471 Avocado	099	/	552 Violet – stamens, peridot lettering
1002	▽	977 Golden brown			
1024	◪	3328 Salmon	1024	/	3328 Salmon – all remaining stitches
328	⊠	3341 Melon	FRENCH KNOT		
1013	✳	3778 Terra-cotta	010	•	351 Coral – gladiolus lettering
			099	•	552 Violet – peridot lettering

Stitch count: 77 high x 31 wide

Finished design size: 4³⁄₈ x 2¹⁄₈ inches

JULY BIRTHDAY JEWELRY BAG

ANCHOR		DMC	ANCHOR		DMC
387	•	Ecru	BACKSTITCH		
1005	⊞	498 Christmas red	1005	/	498 Christmas red – ruby lettering
178	✛	791 Deep cornflower blue	205	/	911 Emerald – stems
177	◆	792 Dark cornflower blue	178	/	791 Deep cornflower blue – all remaining stitches
131	=	798 Delft blue			
205	✳	911 Emerald			

Stitch count: 81 high x 40 wide

Finished design size: 4¹⁄₂ x 2¹⁄₈ inches

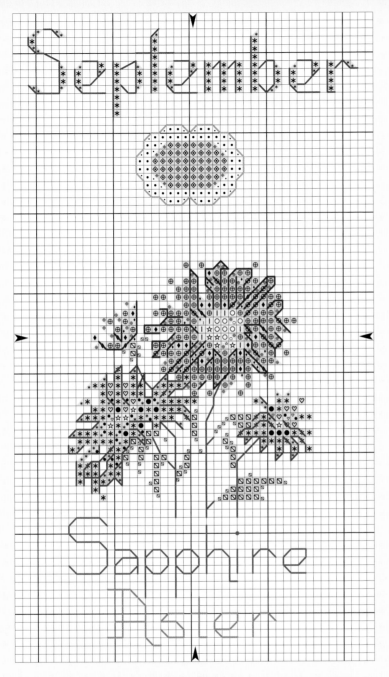

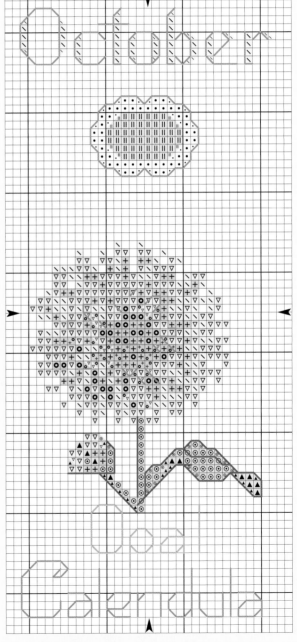

OCTOBER BIRTHDAY JEWELRY BAG

ANCHOR		DMC		ANCHOR		DMC
387	·	Ecru		BACKSTITCH		
217	▲	367 Pistachio		217	/	367 Pistachio – stems, leaves
305	◣	725 Topaz				
035	⊙	891 Carnation		035	/	891 Carnation – October lettering, jewel, flower, calendula lettering
274	‖	928 Gray blue				
298	▽	972 Canary				
262	⊙	3052 Gray green		329	/	3340 Melon – opal lettering
329	⊞	3340 Melon				

Stitch count: 76 high x 33 wide
Finished design size: 4¼ x 1⅞ inches

SEPTEMBER BIRTHDAY JEWELRY BAG

ANCHOR		DMC		ANCHOR		DMC
387	·	Ecru		162	/	517 Wedgwood blue – sapphire lettering
119	◆	333 Deep periwinkle		102	/	550 Violet – flower
253	‖	472 Avocado		1029	/	915 Plum – flowers, September lettering
162	◈	517 Wedgwood blue				
055	♡	604 Cranberry				
295	○	726 Topaz		263	/	3362 Dark loden – stems
302	☆	743 Yellow				
1029	●	915 Plum		087	/	3607 Dark fuchsia – jewel
260	⊡	3364 Light loden				
087	✳	3607 Fuchsia		FRENCH KNOT		
1030	⊕	3746 Dark periwinkle		162	●	517 Wedgwood blue – sapphire lettering
BACKSTITCH						
119	/	333 Deep periwinkle – aster lettering				

Stitch count: 77 high x 43 wide
Finished design size: 4¼ x 2⅜ inches

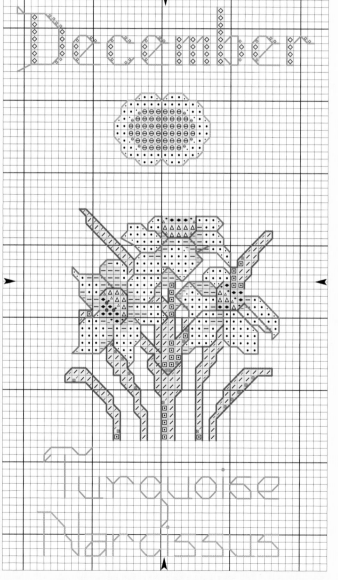

DECEMBER BIRTHDAY JEWELRY BAG

ANCHOR		DMC		ANCHOR		DMC	
387	·	Ecru		333	/	900 Burnt orange – flower centers	
231	−	453 Light shell gray		1002	/	977 Golden brown – jewel, narcissus lettering	
167	◇	598 Turquoise		844	/	3012 Khaki – stems	
168	⊖	807 Peacock blue					
333	◆	900 Burnt orange		**FRENCH KNOT**			
1002	△	977 Golden brown		168	•	807 Peacock blue – turquoise lettering	
844	▣	3012 Khaki		1002	•	977 Golden brown – narcissus lettering	
264	⁄	3348 Yellow green		1028	•	3685 Mauve – flower centers	

BACKSTITCH

232	/	452 Medium shell gray – flowers
168	/	807 Peacock blue – December lettering, turquoise lettering

Stitch count: 76 high x 43 wide

Finished design size: 4¼ x 2³⁄₈ inches

NOVEMBER BIRTHDAY JEWELRY BAG

ANCHOR		DMC		ANCHOR		DMC
387	·	Ecru		**BACKSTITCH**		
1025	♥	347 Salmon		1025	/	347 Salmon – flower
010	□	351 Coral		010	/	351 Coral – jewel, chrysanthemum lettering
214	✗	368 Pistachio				
1047	≡	402 Mahogany		1047	/	402 Mahogany – topaz lettering
681	■	3051 Gray green		681	/	3051 Gray green – November lettering, stems, leaves

Stitch count: 78 high x 46 wide

Finished design size: 4¼ x 2½ inches

The Comforts
of Home

Let your surroundings shine with cross-stitched works of art. This chapter shows you how—with framed pieces for the walls, linens to grace the table, and pillows to perk up any room. Choose from all-time favorite motifs, such as a lighthouse or a rose. Stitching for your home is a wonderful way to bring warmth to the decor and to show off personal style and talent!

This framed piece sings of the warmth and comfort of home. Create the entire sampler, or choose a single motif to stitch on a bread cloth or napkin.

Home Sweet Home

MATERIALS

FABRIC AND FLOSS
14×14-inch piece of 28-count light blue Jubilee
Cotton embroidery floss in colors listed in key

SUPPLIES
Needle; embroidery hoop; desired mat and frame

INSTRUCTIONS

Tape or zigzag fabric edges. Find center of chart and of fabric; begin stitching there. Use three plies of floss to work cross-stitches over two threads of fabric. Work straight stitches and backstitches using one ply. Press stitchery from back. Mat and frame as desired.

ANCHOR		DMC	
002	·	000	White
109	⌐	209	Lavender
1049	★	301	Medium mahogany
400	○	317	True pewter
235	⊠	318	Steel
117	∧	341	Periwinkle
401	■	413	Dark pewter
362	◆	437	Tan
256	○	704	Chartreuse
295	✱	726	Topaz
891	◿	729	Old gold
1060	⟋	747	Sky blue
1022	▽	760	True salmon
379	✳	840	Beige-brown
1044	▲	895	Hunter green
258	‖	904	Parrot green
1023	⌗	3712	Medium salmon
896	●	3721	Shell pink
1048	⊞	3776	Mahogany
386	−	3823	Yellow
176	✕	3839	Lavender-blue
1070	⊕	3849	Teal green
324	⋈	3853	Autumn gold

BACKSTITCH

109	╱	209	Lavender – window trim (1X)
400	╱	317	True pewter – brick house door and roof (1X)
371	╱	433	Chestnut – roof detail (1X)
295	╱	726	Topaz – bird's beak (1X)
1023	╱	3712	Medium salmon – hearts (1X)
386	╱	3823	Yellow – windows (2X)
176	╱	3839	Lavender-blue – birdhouse base (1X); lettering (2X)
401	╱	413	Dark pewter – all remaining stitches (1X)

FRENCH KNOT (1X wrapped twice)

401	●	413	Dark pewter – doorknobs, cat eyes and nose
371	●	433	Chestnut – doorknob, dog eye
295	●	726	Topaz – flowers on shrubs
1022	●	760	True salmon – detail on brick house
258	●	904	Parrot green – potted plant
1023	●	3712	Medium salmon – flowers

Stitch count: 100 high x 100 wide

Finished design sizes:
28-count fabric – 7 x 7 inches
32-count fabric – 6¼ x 6¼ inches
36-count fabric – 5½ x 5½ inches

Family Tree

Stitch this striking family tree in honor of your heritage. Using the alphabet charts on page 145, personalize it with family names and dates as a reference for future generations. This sampler features plaited diagonal square stitches and queen stitches for added interest. The chart for this keepsake is on pages 144–145.

MATERIALS

FABRIC
18×15-inch piece of 28-count French lace linen

FLOSS
Cotton embroidery floss in colors listed in key

SUPPLIES
Needle
Embroidery hoop
Graph paper
Desired frame and mat

INSTRUCTIONS

Tape or zigzag edges of fabric. Find center of chart and of fabric; begin stitching there. Use three plies of floss to work cross-stitches over two threads of fabric. Work backstitches, plaited diagonal square stitches, and queen stitches using two plies.

Chart names and dates using alphabet, *page 145,* separating letters with one square and names with three squares. Position and stitch parents' names, wedding date, stitcher's initials, and year as indicated on chart. Position and stitch children's names as desired. Press and frame.

ANCHOR		DMC
109	⊞	209 Lavender
978	◇	322 Navy
1025	▲	347 Salmon
010	◉	351 Coral
008	⊟	353 Peach
217	●	367 Pistachio
889	■	610 Deep drab brown
898	◩	611 Dark drab brown
832	▣	612 Medium drab brown
243	▽	988 Forest green
264	◪	3348 Yellow green
262	✕	3363 Medium loden
260	⊡	3364 Light loden

BACKSTITCH

360	╱	839 Beige brown–lettering

PLAITED DIAGONAL SQUARE STITCH

109	✳	209 Lavender–border

QUEEN STITCH

109	◈	209 Lavender
978	◈	322 Navy

Stitch count: 173 high x 129 wide

Finished design sizes:
14-count fabric –12³⁄₈ x 9¹⁄₄ inches
12¹⁄₂-count fabric –13⁷⁄₈ x 10³⁄₈ inches
18-count fabric – 9⁵⁄₈ x 7¹⁄₈ inches

Queen Stitch

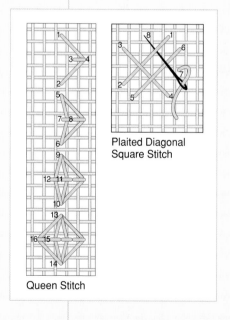

Plaited Diagonal Square Stitch

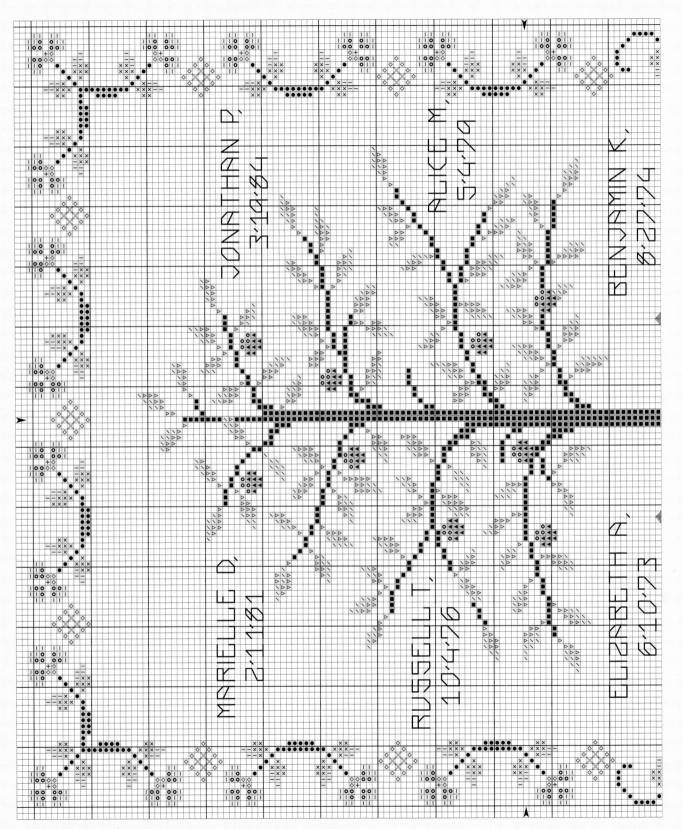

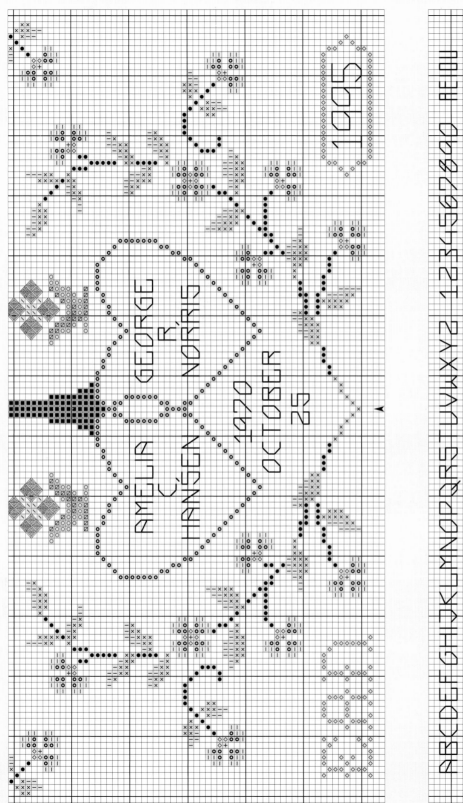

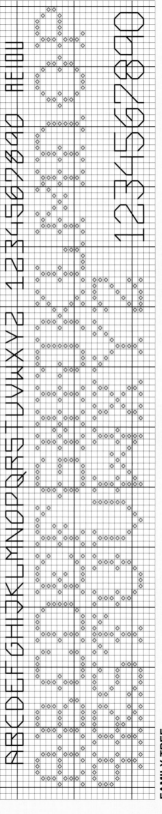

AMELIA GEORGE

C. R.

HANSEN NORRIS

1970

OCTOBER

25

1995

ABCDEFGHIJKLMNOPQRSTUVWXYZ 1234567890 AEIOU

1234567890

FAMILY TREE

Lighthouse by the Sea

Calm waters and cloud-filled skies add to the serene peacefulness of this seascape. Stitched on 25-count Wedgwood Lugana, the lighthouse scene is a welcome addition to any gent's library or office.

MATERIALS

FABRIC
24×20-inch piece of 25-count Wedgwood Lugana fabric

FLOSS
Cotton embroidery floss in colors listed in key

SUPPLIES
Needle; embroidery hoop
Desired mat and frame

INSTRUCTIONS

Tape or zigzag fabric edges to prevent fraying. Find the center of the chart and the center of the fabric; begin stitching there.

Use three plies of floss to work the cross-stitches over two threads of fabric. Work the blended needle as specified in the key. Work the straight stitches using two plies of floss. Work the French knots using one ply of floss. Work the backstitches using one ply of floss unless otherwise specified.

Press the finished stitchery from the back. Mat and frame as desired.

ANCHOR		DMC	
002	•	000	White
897	●	221	Shell pink
403	■	310	Black
399	✶	318	Steel
5975	‖	356	Terra cotta
374	◩	420	Hazel
1042	▯	504	Blue green
280	═	581	True moss green
168	⊞	597	Turquoise
889	◉	610	Deep drab brown
936	✳	632	Deep cocoa
890	☆	729	Old gold
158	−	747	Sky blue
128	△	775	Baby blue
175	⊖	794	Light cornflower blue
169	◆	806	Peacock blue

ANCHOR		DMC	
380	▲	838	Deep beige brown
378	∿	841	True beige brown
848	◯	927	Gray blue
269	◆	936	Pine green
883	◿	3064	Light cocoa
847	◣	3072	Beaver gray
267	⊙	3346	Hunter green
266	✕	3347	Yellow green
263	▼	3362	Dark loden
262	▣	3363	Medium loden
236	◪	3799	Charcoal
069	♥	3803	Mauve
278	▽	3819	Light moss green

BLENDED NEEDLE

361	◿	738	Tan (2X) and
933		543	Pale beige brown (1X)
832	▢	612	Medium drab brown (2X) and
888		3045	Yellow beige (1X)
850	⊞	926	Gray beige (2X) and
848		927	Gray blue (1X)
108	◇	210	Lavender (2X) and
870		3042	Antique violet (1X)

ANCHOR		DMC	
BACKSTITCH			
002	╱	000	White–water
403	╱	310	Black–birds, lighthouse, boat flag, house, rocks, trees (1X)
403	╱	310	Black–top of lighthouse (2X)
924	╱	731	Olive–trees
177	╱	3807	True cornflower blue–boat sails
STRAIGHT STITCH			
002	╱	000	White–boat
069	╱	3803	Mauve–boat
FRENCH KNOT			
403	●	310	Black–top of lighthouse

Stitch count: 158 high x 142 wide
Finished design sizes:
14-count fabric – 11¼ x 10⅛ inches
11-count fabric – 14⅜ x 13 inches

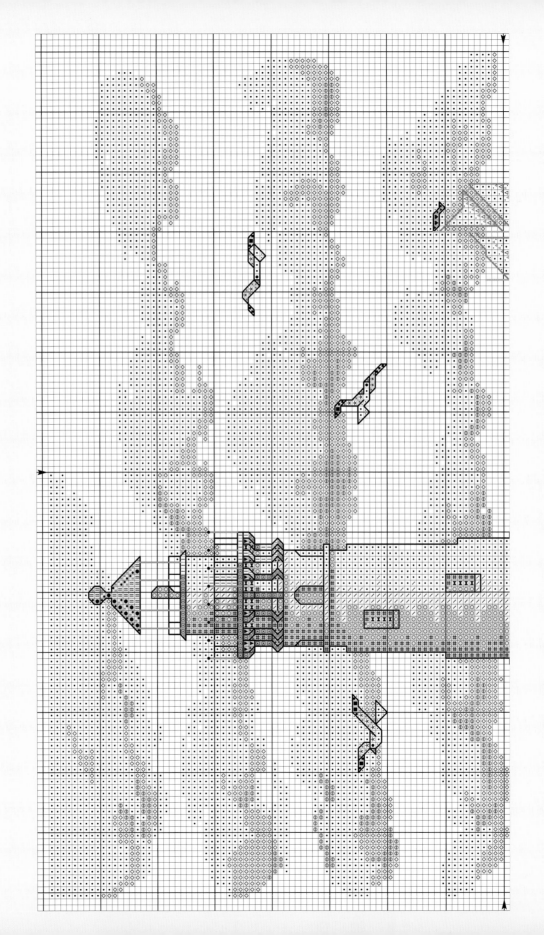

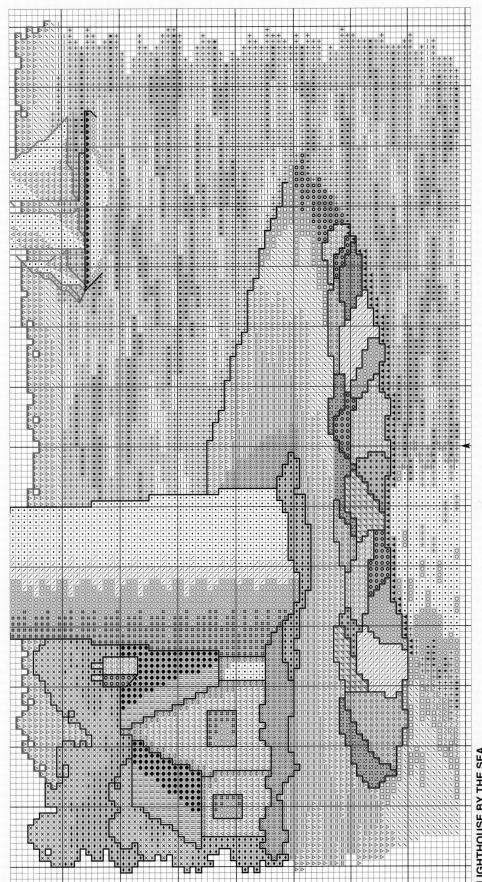

LIGHTHOUSE BY THE SEA

Easter Tea Linens

Set a special Easter table with fine china, a lovely bouquet, and elegant tea linens. The tablecloth and napkins feature a rose-embellished teapot design cross-stitched on 28-count Jubilee fabric. The teapot's rose motif is repeated on the tea cozy, with each rose separated by a lattice of gold thread, machine-stitched over rose floss. Lace edging adds the finishing touch to these heirloom-style tea linens your family will treasure for years. The charts and key are on page 153.

MATERIALS
FOR THE TABLECLOTH AND TWO NAPKINS

FABRIC
1³⁄₄ yards of 55-inch-wide 28-count white Jubilee fabric

FLOSS
Cotton embroidery floss in colors listed in key on page 153
2 additional skeins of DMC 3733
2 spools of gold metallic sewing thread
White sewing thread

SUPPLIES
Needle; embroidery hoop
10 yards of 1-inch-wide flat white lace

INSTRUCTIONS
FOR THE TABLECLOTH AND TWO NAPKINS

Cut a 46¹⁄₂ inch square tablecloth and two 16¹⁄₂ inch square napkins from Jubilee fabric. (Set aside remaining fabric for tea cozy.) Zigzag or serge edges of fabric to prevent fraying. On one corner of each square, measure 1¹⁄₂ inches from edge, and 4 inches from bottom. Begin stitching lower left portion of motif there. Work cross-stitches over two threads of fabric using two plies of floss. Work backstitches using one ply of floss. Repeat the teapot motif in each corner of the tablecloth.

Fold under ¹⁄₄ inch of the zigzagged edges, mitering corners; topstitch. Sew flat lace to under side of stitched hem, mitering lace at corners. Position a six-ply length of floss over stitching; zigzag over floss using gold sewing thread.

MATERIALS
FOR THE TEA COZY

FABRIC
Two 9×11-inch pieces of 28-count white Jubilee fabric
Two 9×11-inch pieces of polyester fleece

Two 9×11-inch pieces white lining fabric

FLOSS
Cotton embroidery floss in colors listed in key, page 153
1 additional skein of DMC 3733
Gold metallic sewing thread
White sewing thread

SUPPLIES
Erasable marker
Needle
Embroidery hoop
¹⁄₄ yard of 1-inch-wide flat white lace
1 yard of ¹⁄₄-inch-wide light pink picot-edged satin ribbon
1 yard of ¹⁄₄-inch-wide rose picot-edged satin ribbon
20-inch piece of ¹⁄₄-inch-wide elastic
2 purchased 2³⁄₄-inch-long white tassels

INSTRUCTIONS
FOR THE TEA COZY

Zigzag or serge edges of Jubilee fabric pieces to prevent fraying. Using erasable marker, draw a 2-inch-wide grid of diagonal squares centered on each piece of Jubilee fabric.

For front, with a long edge at top, find the center of one

continued on page 152

square and the center of chart; begin stitching a rose motif there.

Work all cross-stitches using two plies of floss over two threads of fabric. Work backstitches using one ply of floss. Repeat rose motif in center of each complete square on grid. For back, with a long edge at top, stitch one rose motif in only the center square.

Baste a piece of fleece to wrong side of each piece of Jubilee fabric. Lay a six-ply length of floss over each line of grid; machine-zigzag over floss using gold thread. Repeat for each line of marked grid. Erase marker lines.

For side seams, on wrong side of front, measure and mark the point 2 inches from the bottom on both sides. Measure and mark the point 2 inches from the top edge on left side only. With right sides facing, sew front and back together using ½-inch seam allowances and stitching from marked point to the top or bottom edge. Press seams open and turn right side out. Sew lining pieces in the same manner. Press seams open, but do not turn.

Baste straight edge of lace ⅜ inch from top edge of Jubilee fabric with right sides facing. With right sides facing, sew Jubilee fabric and lining together along top edge, catching in edge of lace. Sew bottom edge and both sides of slit (handle opening) on right side. Turn and press.

For bottom casing, stitch around the bottom edge ½ inch from seam line. Open one lining seam between the bottom seam and the casing stitching. Insert elastic into the bottom casing.

Slip cozy over teapot. Adjust fit of elastic, remove cozy, and secure ends. Sew lining opening closed.

For top casing, stitch around the top edge, ½ inch from seam line. Hand-sew lining to Jubilee fabric along side (spout) opening below casing stitching.

Insert both ribbons through top casing. Place cozy on teapot; pull ribbons to tighten and tie into a bow. Adjust gathers evenly. Tack tassels just below ribbon ties.

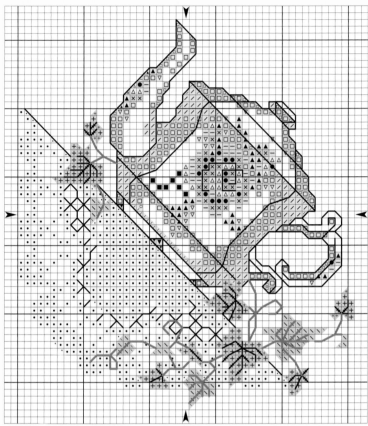

EASTER TEA LINENS

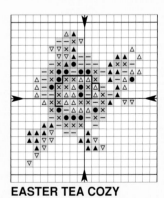

EASTER TEA COZY

EASTER TEA LINENS AND COZY		
ANCHOR		DMC
399	⟋	318 Steel
217	▲	367 Medium pistachio
214	▽	368 Light pistachio
398	▢	415 Pearl gray
860	+	522 Dark olive drab
858	⟍	524 Light olive drab
392	■	642 Beige gray
885	•	739 Tan
073	△	963 Pale rose pink
059	●	3350 Deep dusty rose
076	⊠	3731 Dark dusty rose
075	—	3733 Medium dusty rose
236	▼	3799 Dark charcoal

BACKSTITCH

218	⟋	319 Dark pistachio – veins of dark leaves
217	⟋	367 Medium pistachio – veins of light leaves, vines
401	⟋	413 Pewter – rose, teapot detail
885	⟋	739 Tan (2X) – doily
236	⟋	3799 Dark charcoal – teapot outline, table edge

TEA LINENS stitch count: 57 high x 51 wide

TEA LINENS finished design sizes:
14-count fabric – 4 x 3⅝ inches
11-count fabric – 5⅛ x 4⅝ inches
18-count fabric – 3⅛ x 2⅞ inches

TEA COZY stitch count: 18 high x 16 wide

TEA COZY finished design sizes:
14-count fabric – 1¼ x 1⅛ inches
11-count fabric – 1⅝ x 1½ inches
18-count fabric – 1 x ⅞ inches

Victorian Bouquets

Brighten any room with flowers, especially the cross-stitched everlasting variety. These colorful blooms are beautiful on a box lid, as a napkin, or stitched as a pillow front. The charts and key are on pages 156–157.

MATERIALS
FOR THE NAPKIN

FABRIC
16×16-inch piece of 28-count ivory Jobelan fabric

FLOSS
Cotton embroidery floss in colors listed in key
Gold lamé thread

SUPPLIES
Needle; embroidery hoop; 2 yards of gold cable

INSTRUCTIONS
FOR THE NAPKIN

Tape or zigzag fabric edges. Begin stitching 1 inch from both edges on one corner of the fabric. Use three plies of floss to work the cross-stitches over two threads of fabric. Work the French knots as specified in key. Work backstitches using one ply.

To finish the linen, trim the napkin size to 15½ inches square with design 1 inch in from corner. Use one strand of gold lamé thread to machine-zigzag over the gold cable ⅝ inch in from the outer edge. Fringe the napkin ½ inch.

MATERIALS
FOR THE BOX

FABRIC
13×13-inch piece of 28-count ivory Jobelan fabric

FLOSS
Cotton embroidery floss in colors listed in key

SUPPLIES
Needle; embroidery hoop
Purchased 7×7-inch box with a 5¼×5¼-inch opening

INSTRUCTIONS
FOR THE BOX

Tape or zigzag fabric edges. Find the center of the chart and of fabric; begin stitching there. Use three plies of floss to work the cross-stitches over two threads of fabric. Work the French knots as specified in the key. Work backstitches using one ply of floss.

Press the stitchery from the back. Insert stitchery into the box following the manufacturer's instructions.

continued on page 156

MATERIALS
FOR THE PILLOW

FABRIC
15×15-inch piece of 10-count cream Heatherfield fabric

FLOSS
Cotton embroidery floss in colors listed in key

SUPPLIES
Needle; embroidery hoop; 1¼ yards pink taffeta
1½ yards piping cord
12½×12½-inch piece of underlining fabric
12½×12½-inch piece of fusible interfacing; 10-inch pillow form

INSTRUCTIONS
FOR THE PILLOW

Tape or zigzag fabric edges. Find center of chart and fabric; begin stitching there. Working over two threads, use four plies of floss for cross-stitches and two plies for backstitches. Work the French knots as listed in key. To finish the pillow, use ½-inch seam allowances and stitch seams right sides facing unless otherwise specified. Keeping design centered, cut fabric into a 12½ inch square and baste underlining fabric to the wrong side.

For ruffle, cut 7-inch-wide bias fabric strips, seaming as necessary, for a total of 96 inches. Press ruffle in half lengthwise with wrong sides facing. Sew a gathering thread through both layers of ruffle ½-inch from raw edges. Pull threads to fit perimeter of pillow front with raw edges even; adjust gathers evenly. Cut a 1½×50-inch bias strip and cover piping cord. Use a zipper foot to sew through both fabric layers close to cording. Pin cording to pillow front, raw edges even. Cut backing fabric in same manner as front. Fuse interfacing to wrong side of backing fabric.

Pin piping and ruffle strip around outside edge of pillow front, keeping raw edges even. Stitch in place. With right sides together, stitch pillow front to back, leaving an opening for turning. Trim corners. Turn right side out. Insert pillow form. Sew opening closed.

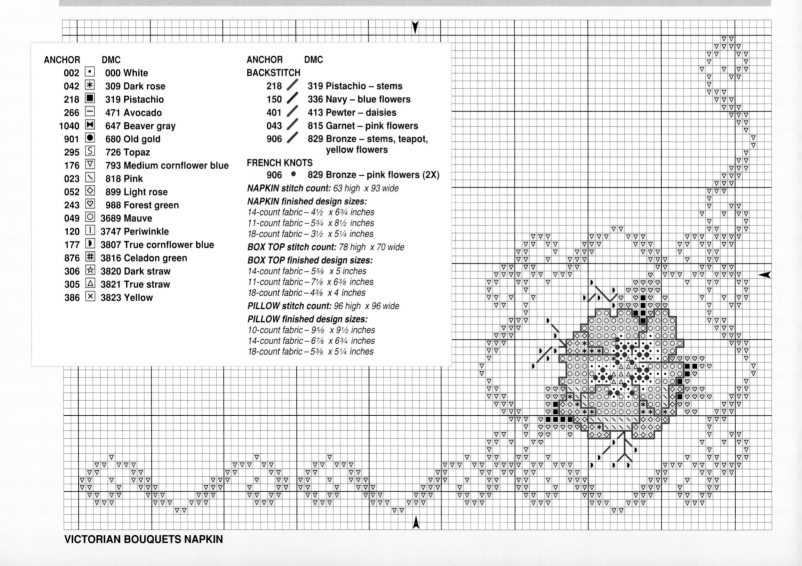

ANCHOR		DMC	
002	·	000	White
042	✳	309	Dark rose
218	■	319	Pistachio
266	−	471	Avocado
1040	⋈	647	Beaver gray
901	●	680	Old gold
295	S	726	Topaz
176	▽	793	Medium cornflower blue
023	◺	818	Pink
052	⬡	899	Light rose
243	♡	988	Forest green
049	◎	3689	Mauve
120	❘	3747	Periwinkle
177	◗	3807	True cornflower blue
876	⌗	3816	Celadon green
306	☆	3820	Dark straw
305	△	3821	True straw
386	✕	3823	Yellow

ANCHOR		DMC	
BACKSTITCH			
218	╱	319	Pistachio – stems
150	╱	336	Navy – blue flowers
401	╱	413	Pewter – daisies
043	╱	815	Garnet – pink flowers
906	╱	829	Bronze – stems, teapot, yellow flowers
FRENCH KNOTS			
906	●	829	Bronze – pink flowers (2X)

NAPKIN stitch count: 63 high x 93 wide
NAPKIN finished design sizes:
14-count fabric – 4½ x 6¾ inches
11-count fabric – 5¾ x 8½ inches
18-count fabric – 3½ x 5¼ inches

BOX TOP stitch count: 78 high x 70 wide
BOX TOP finished design sizes:
14-count fabric – 5⅝ x 5 inches
11-count fabric – 7⅛ x 6⅜ inches
18-count fabric – 4⅜ x 4 inches

PILLOW stitch count: 96 high x 96 wide
PILLOW finished design sizes:
10-count fabric – 9⅝ x 9½ inches
14-count fabric – 6⅞ x 6¾ inches
18-count fabric – 5⅜ x 5¼ inches

VICTORIAN BOUQUETS NAPKIN

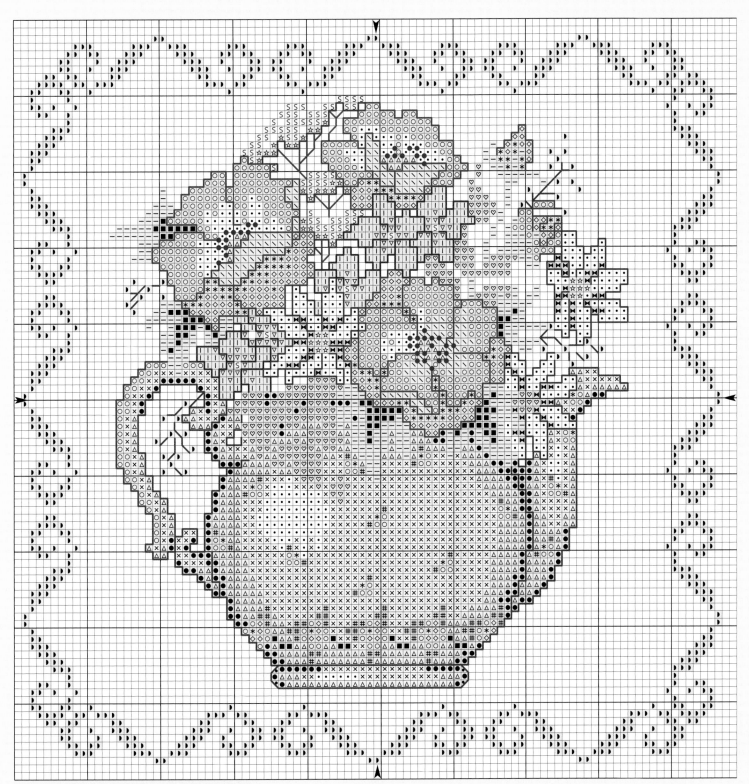

VICTORIAN BOUQUETS PILLOW AND BOX TOP

My Heart Sings Sampler

A lacy trellis of Smyrna crosses and a curving spray of tender pink roses frame this charming verse about stitching. Three hearts filled with specialty stitches and a sprinkling of dainty seed beads add a delicate finishing touch to this sampler. The design is a perfect project for brushing up on your stitching skills or for learning some new stitches. Complete chart and key are on pages 160–161.

MATERIALS

FABRIC
18×15-inch piece of 28-count tea-dyed Monaco fabric

FLOSS
Cotton embroidery floss in colors listed in key on page 161
Blending filament in colors listed in key on page 161

SUPPLIES
Needle; embroidery hoop
Seed beads in color listed in key on page 161
Desired frame and mat

INSTRUCTIONS

Tape or zigzag fabric edges. Find the vertical center of the chart and the vertical center of the fabric. Measure three inches from the top of fabric; begin stitching the top row of flowers there.

Use three plies of floss to work all cross-stitches over two threads of fabric before working specialty stitches. Work blended needle as specified in key. Work backstitches using one ply of floss. Use two plies of floss to work Smyrna cross-stitches.

For left heart, work the left-slanting rows of reverse Scotch stitch using four plies of floss as in the diagram, *below.* Turn fabric and work the remaining rows of reverse Scotch stitch in the opposite direction using four plies.

For center heart, work diamond eyelet stitches using two plies of floss and referring to diagram *below.* Give each stitch a gentle tug to open a small hole in center of each eyelet.

For right heart, work satin stitches using four plies of floss and referring to diagram *below.*

Use one ply of pale rose (DMC 3326) floss to sew beads to positions indicated on chart. Press stitchery from the back and frame as desired.

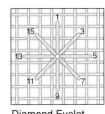

Diamond Eyelet

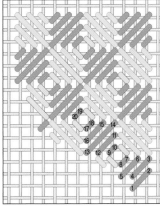

Reverse Scotch Stitch

Satin Stitch

Smyrna Cross-Stitch

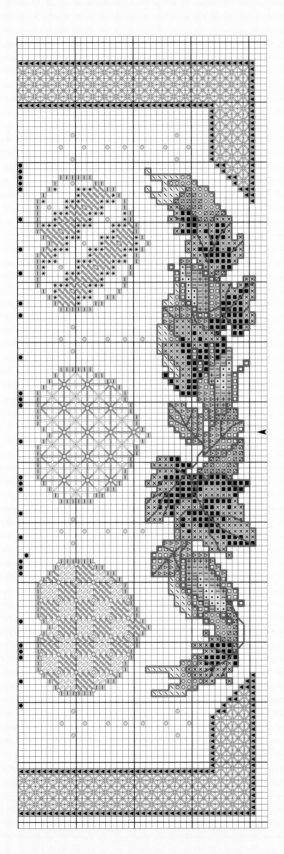

MY HEART SINGS SAMPLER

ANCHOR	DMC	
979	●	312 Navy
218	■	890 Pistachio
052	I	899 Light rose
246	✕	986 Forest green
036	✻	3326 Pale rose
267	▽	3346 Hunter green
264	☐	3348 Yellow green
393	◀	3790 Beige gray

BLENDED NEEDLE

059	✚	326 Deep rose (2X) and
		031 Kreinik crimson
		blending filament (2X)

ANCHOR	DMC	
BLENDED NEEDLE		
038	▬	335 Medium rose (2X) and
		031 Kreinik crimson
		blending filament (2X)
1038	◯	519 Dark sky blue (2X) and
		006 Kreinik blue
		blending filament (2X)
158	◩	747 Light sky blue (2X) and
		094 Kreinik star blue
		blending filament (2X)
169	◪	806 Peacock blue (2X) and
		006 Kreinik blue
		blending filament (2X)

ANCHOR	DMC	
BLENDED NEEDLE		
036	•	3326 Pale rose (2X) and
		007 Kreinik pink
		blending filament (2X)

BACKSTITCH

1005	╱	816 Garnet—roses
1050	╱	3781 Dark mocha—verse
	╱	009 Kreinik emerald
		blending filament—
		ivy and rose leaves
	╱	033 Kreinik royal
		blending filament—
		ribbons

ANCHOR	DMC	
SATIN STITCH		
052	▨	899 Light rose
REVERSE SCOTCH STITCH		
052	▨	899 Light rose
036	▨	3326 Pale rose
DIAMOND EYELET STITCH		
052	✳	899 Light rose
036	✳	3326 Pale rose
SMYRNA CROSS-STITCH		
903	✳	3032 Medium mocha
BEADS		
	⦿	00145 Mill Hill pink
		seed beads

Stitch count: 151 high x 128 wide

Finished design sizes:
14-count fabric—10¾ x 9⅛ inches
16-count fabric—9½ x 8 inches
12½-count fabric—12⅛ x 10¼ inches

Cross-Stitch Basics

GETTING STARTED

Cut floss into 15- to 18-inch lengths and separate all six plies. Recombine plies as indicated in project instructions and thread into a blunt-tip needle. Rely on project instructions to find out where to begin stitching.

BASIC CROSS-STITCH

Make one cross-stitch for each symbol on chart. For horizontal rows, stitch the first diagonal of each stitch in the row. Work back across row, completing each stitch. On most linen and even-weave fabrics, stitches are usually worked over two threads as shown in the diagrams, *below.* Each stitch fills one square on Aida cloth.

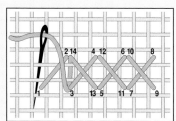

Basic Cross-Stitch in Rows

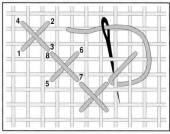

Basic Cross-Stitch Worked Individually

Cross-stitches also can be worked in the reverse direction; just remember to embroider the stitches uniformly. That is, always work the top half of the stitch in the same direction.

HOW TO SECURE THREAD AT BEGINNING

The most common way to secure the beginning tail of thread is to hold it under the first four or five stitches.

Or you can use a waste knot. Thread needle and knot end of thread. Insert needle from right side of fabric, about 4 inches from placement of first stitch. Bring needle up through fabric and work first series of stitches. When stitching is finished, turn piece to right side and clip the knot. Rethread needle with excess floss and push needle through to the wrong side of stitchery.

When you work with two, four, or six plies of floss, use a loop knot. Cut half as many plies of thread, and make each one twice as long. Recombine plies, fold the strand in half, and thread all the ends into the needle. Work the first diagonal of the first stitch, then slip the needle through the loop formed by folding the thread.

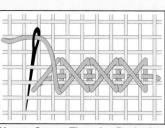

How to Secure Thread at Beginning

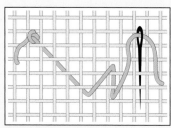

Waste Knot

HOW TO SECURE THREAD AT END

To finish, slip threaded needle under previously stitched threads on wrong side of fabric for four or five stitches, weaving thread back and forth a few times. Clip thread.

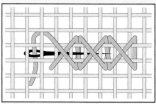

How to Secure Thread at End

HALF STITCHES

A half cross-stitch is a single diagonal or half of a cross-stitch. Half cross-stitches usually are listed under a separate heading in the color key and are indicated on the chart by a diagonal colored line in the desired direction.

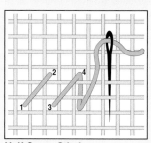

Half Cross-Stitch

QUARTER AND THREE-QUARTER STITCHES

Quarter and three-quarter cross-stitches are used to obtain rounded shapes in a design. On linen and even-weave fabrics, a quarter stitch extends from the corner to the center intersection of threads. To make quarter stitches on Aida cloth, estimate the center of the square. Three-quarter stitches combine a quarter stitch with a half cross-stitch. Both of these stitches may slant in any direction.

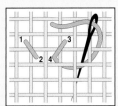

Quarter Cross-Stitch

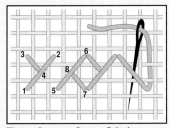

Three-Quarter Cross-Stitch

CROSS-STITCHES WITH BEADS

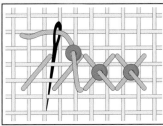

Cross-Stitch with Bead

When beads are attached using a cross-stitch, work half cross-stitches and attach beads on the return stitch.

BACKSTITCHES

Backstitches define and outline the shapes in a design. For most cross-stitch projects, backstitches require only one ply of floss. On the color key, (2X) indicates two plies of floss, (3X) indicates three plies, etc.

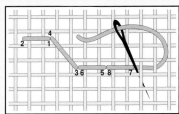

Backstitch

FRENCH KNOTS

Bring threaded needle through fabric and wrap floss around the needle as illustrated. Tighten the twists and insert needle back through the same place in the fabric. The floss will slide through the wrapped thread to make the knot.

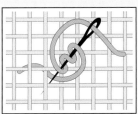

French Knot

WHIPSTITCHES

A whipstitch is an overcast stitch that often is used to finish edges on projects that use perforated plastic. The stitches are pulled tightly for a neatly finished edge. Whipstitches also can be used to join two fabrics.

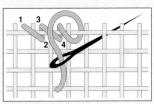

Whipstitch

continued on page 164

FEATHERSTITCHES

This decorative stitch produces a featherlike shape as long or as short as desired. Bring threaded needle to front at top of feather. Insert needle back into fabric approximately four threads away, leaving stitch loose. Bring needle to front again, slightly lower than center of first stitch; catch thread from first stitch. Repeat in an alternating motion until desired length is achieved. End feather by stitching a straight-stitched quill.

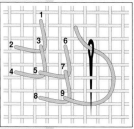

Featherstitch

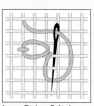

Lazy Daisy Stitch

LAZY DAISY STITCHES

To make this petal-shaped stitch, bring the needle to the front. Using a sewing-style stitch, insert the needle back through the same hole and out again two or more threads away, catching the loop under the needle. Gently pull to shape the loop. Push the needle back through the fabric on the other side of the loop to tack the loop in place.

MATERIAL FOR CROSS-STITCH

Counted cross-stitch has become a popular form of stitchery. Many stitchers like to work cross-stitch designs on different fabrics and use threads different than specified in the projects. The following information will help you understand and adapt the projects in this book.

CROSS-STITCH FABRICS

Counted cross-stitch can be worked on any fabric that will enable you to make consistently sized, even stitches.

Aida cloth is the most popular of all cross-stitch fabrics. Threads are woven in groups separated by tiny spaces. This creates a pattern of squares across the surface of fabric and enables a beginning stitcher to easily identify where cross-stitches should be placed. Aida cloth is measured by squares per inch; 14-count Aida cloth has 14 squares per inch.

Aida cloth comes in many varieties. Aida cloth that is 100 percent cotton is available in thread counts 6, 8, 11, 14, 16, and 18. Fourteen-count cotton Aida cloth is available in more than 60 colors. For beginners, white Aida cloth is available with a removable grid of prebasted threads.

Linen is considered to be the standard of excellence for experienced stitchers. The threads used to weave linen vary in diameter, giving linen fabrics a slightly irregular surface. When you purchase linen, remember that the thread count is measured by threads per inch, and most designs are worked over two threads, so 28-count linen will yield 14 stitches per inch. Linens are made in counts from 14 (seven stitches per inch) to 40.

Even-weave fabric also is worked over two threads. The popularity of cross-stitch has created a market for specialty fabrics for counted cross-stitch. They are referred to as even-weave fabrics because they are woven from threads with a consistent diameter, even though some of these fabrics are woven to create a homespun look. Most even-weave fabrics are counted as linen is counted, by threads per inch, and worked over two threads.

Hardanger fabric can be used for very fine counted cross-stitch. The traditional fabric for the Norwegian embroidery of the same name has an over-two, under-two weave that produces 22 small squares per inch.

Needlepoint canvas is frequently used for cross-stitching, especially on clothing and other fabrics that are not suitable alone. Waste canvas is designed to unravel when dampened. It ranges in count from 6½ to 20 stitches per inch. Cross-stitches also can be worked directly on mono-needlepoint canvas. This is available in colors, and when the background is left unstitched, it can create an interesting effect.

Sweaters and other knits often are worked in duplicate

Fabric/Needle/Floss

FABRIC	TAPESTRY NEEDLE SIZE	NUMBER OF PLIES
11-count	24	three
14-count	24–26	two or three
18-count	26	two
22-count	26	one

stitch from cross-stitch charts. Knit stitches are not square; they are wider than they are tall. A duplicate-stitched design will appear broader and shorter than the chart.

Gingham or other simple plaid fabrics can be used, but gingham "squares" are not perfectly square, so a stitched design will seem slightly taller and narrower than the chart.

Burlap fabric can easily be counted and stitched over as you would a traditional counted-thread fabric.

THREADS FOR STITCHING

Most types of threads available for embroidery can be used for counted cross-stitch projects.

Six-ply cotton embroidery floss is available in the widest range of colors, including variegated ones. Six-ply floss is made to be separated easily into single or multiple plies for stitching. Instructions with each project in this book tell you how many plies to use. A greater number of plies will result in an embroidered piece that is rich or heavy; few plies will create a lightweight or fragile texture.

Rayon or silk floss is similar in weight to cotton floss, but the stitches have a greater sheen. Either thread can be exchanged with cotton floss, one ply for one ply, but because they have a "slicker" texture, they are slightly more difficult to use.

Pearl cotton is available in four sizes: #3, #5, #8, and #12 (#3 is thick; #12 is thin). It has an obvious twist and a high sheen.

Flower thread is a 100 percent cotton, matte-finish thread. A single strand of flower thread can be substituted for two plies of cotton floss.

Overdyed threads are being introduced on the market every day. Most of them have an irregularly variegated, one-of-a-kind appearance. Cotton floss, silk floss, flower thread, and pearl cotton weight threads are available in this form. All of them produce a soft, shaded appearance without changing thread colors.

Specialty threads can add a distinctive look to cross-stitch. They range in weight from hair-fine blending filament, usually used with floss, to ⅛-inch-wide ribbon. They include numerous metallic threads, richly colored and textured threads, and fun-to-stitch glow-in-the-dark threads.

Wool yarn, usually used for needlepoint or crewel embroidery, can be used for cross-stitch. Use one or two plies of three-ply Persian yarn. Select even-weave fabrics with fewer threads per inch when working cross-stitches in wool yarn.

Ribbon in silk, rayon, and polyester becomes an interesting texture for cross-stitching, especially in combination with flower-shape stitches. Look for straight-grain and bias-cut ribbons in solid and variegated colors and in widths from ¹⁄₁₆ to 1½ inches.

TYPES OF NEEDLES

Blunt-point needles are best for working on most cross-stitch fabrics because they slide through holes and between threads without splitting or snagging the fibers. A large-eye needle accommodates the bulk of embroidery threads. Many companies sell needles labeled "cross-stitch," and they are identical to tapestry needles, blunt-tip, and large-eye. The chart, *above,* will guide you to the right size needle for most common fabrics. One exception to the blunt-tip needle rule is waste canvas; use sharp embroidery needles to poke through that fabric.

Working with seed beads requires a very fine needle to slide through the holes. A #8 quilting needle, which is short with a tiny eye, and a long beading needle with a longer eye are readily available. Some shops carry short beading needles with a long eye.

Cross-Stitch Tips

PREPARING FABRIC

The edges of cross-stitch fabric take a lot of abrasion while a project is being stitched. There are many ways to keep fabric from fraying while you stitch.

The easiest and most widely available method is to bind the edges with masking tape. Because tape leaves a residue that's almost impossible to remove, it should be trimmed away after stitching is completed. All projects in this book that include tape in the instructions were planned with a large margin around the stitched fabric so the tape can be trimmed away.

There are some projects where you should avoid using masking tape. If a project does not allow for ample margins to trim away the tape, use one of these techniques: If you have a sewing machine available, zigzag stitching, serging, and narrow hemming are all neat and effective methods. Hand-overcasting also works well, but it is more time-consuming.

Garments, table linens, towels, and other projects that will be washed on a regular basis when they are finished should be washed before stitching to avoid shrinkage later. Wash the fabric in the same manner you will wash the finished project.

PREPARING FLOSS

Most cotton embroidery floss is colorfast and won't fade. A few bright colors, notably reds and greens, contain excess dye that could bleed onto fabrics if dampened. To remove the excess dye before stitching, gently slip off paper bands from floss and rinse each color in cool water until the water rinses clear. Place floss on white paper towels to dry. If there is any color on the towels when the floss is dried, repeat the process. When completely dry, slip the paper bands back on the floss.

CENTERING THE DESIGN

Most of the projects in this book instruct you to begin stitching at the center of the chart and fabric. To find the center of the chart, follow the horizontal and vertical arrows on the chart to the point where they intersect.

To find the center of the fabric you're using, fold the fabric in half horizontally and baste along the fold. Then fold the fabric in half vertically and baste along the fold. The point where the basting intersects is the center of the fabric. Some stitchers add additional lines of basting every 10 or 20 rows as a stitching guide.

CLEANING YOUR WORK

You may want to wash your needlecraft pieces before mounting and framing them because the natural oils from your hands eventually will discolor the stitchery. Wash your piece by hand in cool water using mild detergent. Rinse several times until the water is clear.

Do not wring or squeeze the needlecraft piece to remove the water. Hold the piece over the sink until dripping slows, then place it flat on a clean terry-cloth towel, and roll tightly. Unroll the stitchery and lay flat to dry.

PRESSING YOUR WORK

Using a warm iron, carefully press the fabric from the back before framing or finishing it. If the piece has lots of surface texture stitches, place it on a terry-cloth towel or other padded surface to press.

FRAMING YOUR DESIGN

Use determines how cross-stitch pieces should be mounted and framed. Needlework shops, professional framers, and crafts stores offer many options.

For most purposes, omit the glass when framing cross-stitch. Moisture can build up between the glass and the stitchery, and sunlight is intensified by the glass. Both can cause damage to the fabric. If you must use glass, be sure to mat the piece so the stitchery does not touch the glass.

Index

Index—continued

Sources

CROSS-STITCH FABRIC

Wichelt Imports, Inc.
N162 Hwy. 35
Stoddard, WI 54658

Zweigart
262 Old New Brunswick
  Road
Piscataway, NJ 08854
908–271–1949

EMBROIDERY FLOSS

Anchor
Consumer Service
  Department
P.O. Box 27067
Greenville, SC 29616

DMC
Port Kearney Building 10
South Kearney, NJ
  07032-0650

BEADS

Gay Bowles Sales/Mill Hill
P.O. Box 1060
Janesville, WI 53547
www.millhill.com
800–356–9438

Westrim Trimming
Corporation at
  9667 Cantoga Avenue
Chatsworth, CA 91331
www.westrimcrafts.com
818–998–8550

Bodacious Beads
1942 River Road
Des Plaines, IL 84769-7959

RIBBON

CM Offray & Son Inc.
Route 24, Box 601
Chester, NJ 07930-0601
908–879–4700